Decr Your Today!

DECREE A THING
AND IT SHALL
BE ESTABLISHED

In this book you will learn how to decree your today to establish your tomorrow. Decree His Kingdom by the words you speak each and everyday!

by Brent L Luck

Foreword by Dennis Walker

Author Contact:
Eternal Purpose, Maricopa, Arizona
www.brentlluck.com - brentluck@gmail.com

Published by XP Publishing (A ministry of XP Ministries)
PO Box 1017,
Maricopa AZ 85139
xpministries.com

ISBN 978-1621661-65-8

ENDORSEMENTS

One profound truth I discovered during the countless times Holy Spirit has caught me up to Heaven was the importance of using our words to declare and decree! When God spoke, it WAS and whatever He called forth, it CAME and all those present in that spiritual world called Heaven could both hear and see the frequency of His voice. Once His words were released, things began to form and shift and creation would take place, He has made us in that same image and after His likeness (how He operates) and gave us the power of Life and Death in our tongue. It is truly one of our most powerful resources, and when our words are released through declarations of praise, of faith and with authority, it sends shockwaves through the spirit realm and we begin to move things instead of things moving us. We begin to MANIFEST the Will and Ways of the Father and life will never be the same again. I highly recommend this powerful book that Brent has written with Holy Spirit and suggest you draw from and apply the revelations found therein. My own life is proof that when you declare the words of God continually, His presence, His life, His love and His power flow through you and darkness runs to get out of your way. You become aflame as Heaven begins to pour into your atmosphere and you begin to work together with the one who made you to establish His Kingdom on earth!

Kat Kerr
Author of *Revealing Heaven*

The Universe is framed by the Word of God according to Hebrews 11:3. Brent Luck's book is a life changing, valuable prophetic tool to be used by every believer. **Decreeing Your Today** is a powerful, profound way to change your circumstances by aligning your spirit, soul and body to Heavens truth. *Decree Your Today* will teach you to speak and receive the promises in Word of God.

Pastor Carl Garitson
Solid Rock Church Sedona, AZ

Brent is an amazing gift to the Kingdom. I have known Brent for several years and have ministered with him many times. He is a great friend of mine and truly a friend of the Lord. This book will be a blessing and will inspire you -a true DECREE of the heart.

Wendell Mcgowan
Itinerate speaker

Decree Your Today is a fresh look into ancient wisdom. Get a hold of these truths and watch the miraculous power and favor of God begin to flow into your life and the lives of others! Brent's ministry has been marked not only by prophetic insight and the miraculous, but also his deep love and passion for the presence of the Lord is very contagious. It has been said that true prophets will draw you closer to the Heart of God, and this is truly what my friend Brent's life does. It is an honor to call him my friend!

Michael Leyde
Worship Pastor, ICLV.

TABLE OF CONTENTS

Acknowledgments 7

Foreword 9

A Personal Story 11

Preface 13

Introduction 17

1 Decree and Declare to Establish 25

2 My Heavenly Nuggets & Insights 29

3 Let Us Decree a Thing 33

4 Decrees for Wisdom 39

5 Quick Start Declarations for Today 41

6 Now! Decree Your Today 45

7 Prophetic Downloads & Power Decrees 51

8 Life or Death 57

9 Righteous Decrees & Victorious Declarations 65

10 Decrees for Healing 69

11 The Comma and the Standard 83

12 Decree with Absolute Faith 89

13 Decree to Know and Manifest 95

14 In Jesus' Name I Am 101

15 Heart Decrees of Passion & Fire 109

16 According to Your Word 125

17 Decree Psalm 91 129

18 Decree Ephesians 1 131

19 Decrees of Power & Scripture 133

20 I Am In Christ 143

21 I Decree He Is 147

22 Hallowing the Names of God 153

23 Decreeing the One Another Scriptures 161

24 I Am & I Have 167

25 Decrees for Favor 173

26 Everyday Decrees and Declarations 191

27 Decrees to Tear Down Strongholds 185

28 Decree as A Child of God 187

29 Decrees of His Word & His Goodness 193

30 Decrees for Prosperity & Provision 199

31 Decrees As an Overcomer 203

32 Decrees of Life 209

33 Decree and Pray Isaiah 61 215

34 Decree Your Dream Today 221

35 My Final Thought 225

ACKNOWLEDGMENTS

This book is first and foremost dedicated to the Father and His voice. Everything in this book is meant to bring you not just closer to the heart of God, but that we will know and speak His heart to the world and change the world.

I also dedicate this book to my wonderful wife Melissa, who is also known as 'Princess"! She is a true Proverbs 31 woman of God with His heart. She is my love, my song, my dance, my business partner and favorite person in life. I get to spend almost every hour of every day with her.

Also my three wonderful children Devin, Zofia and Samantha who constantly remind me how important your child's love is. My kids always encourage me by hugs, sloppy kisses and hand rubs that only your children can give you.

To Apostle Dennis and Lynnie Walker and all of our Dunamis family. You saw who I was and were not afraid of what you saw. You unwrapped me and called me a gift!

To Dr. Bob Cathers our first Apostle, you have been with us from the beginning. We thank you for your love and the revelation of righteousness which has changed us forever. Melissa and I love you and appreciate your care for us. You have been a rock of support for us!

A very special embrace to my friends Jim and Marcella Wies for helping this book take flight and land in the hearts of believers and to the world. Thanks as well to Charles Franklin Linn for editorial help with grammar.

To all my Spirit led friends and heavenly family thank you for being apart of my life.

Finally to all of you who will begin to speak these decrees into the earth on a daily basis preparing the way for the coming of this next move of God!

FOREWORD

God created Adam and Eve in His image. We have many attributes that reflect the divine attributes of God. God as the creator of all things has made us to be creative as well. God's chief means of creating was to speak and it was so. We have been given the same ability to speak and be creative, but take heed what you declare. I think it is obvious to us that our words are powerful agents of change in the atmosphere around us. This is what makes worship so powerful to bring us into the very atmosphere of Heaven. God is enthroned on the praises of His people. I believe that the authority God gave to Adam and Eve to care for their garden was the power of decree! (There were no weed whackers in the Garden of Eden and Adam didn't work by the sweat of his brow until after the fall.)

I believe that this awesome power of decreeing and declaring is still available for us today as we follow the promptings of the Holy Spirit. I personally am thankful that not every word that has ever come out of my mouth is that powerful. But when our words, decrees and declarations are aligned with the words of God, real power is unleashed. After all, "man shall not live by bread alone, but by every word that proceeds from the mouth of God." We serve a God who spoke in times past to the prophets, and who is still speaking to us today. We just need to set our hearts and minds on the one who loved us so much that He gave His life for us. He has the words of life and He wants to fill our mouth with those words, to release His recreating power on our life and the lives of those around us.

I have watched my friend and fellow laborer Brent Luck step into this role of becoming the mouthpiece of God. "Let everyone who speaks, speak as the oracle of God." I have seen Brent grow in this prophetic ability, and I have had the honor and pleasure of serving alongside of him at Dunamis Apostolic Resource Center in Las Vegas, Nevada. What this lets me know is that these things are available to all those who believe. Brent is being made into a forerunner and example of where God wants to take us all. We are all called to speak the very heart of the Father over our environment and watch as recreation takes place. At Dunamis we call this "Catching the Initiatives of Heaven."

Dennis Walker
Living Epistle

A PERSONAL STORY

While writing and compiling this book a frightening and yet amazing thing happened that showed me just how important these decrees are.

On September 8, 2013, at around two o'clock. I found my four-year-old daughter Samantha lying on the couch unresponsive. Her face was blue and I could tell something was seriously wrong. I immediately picked her up, started shaking her and spoke life into her. I started yelling and commanding life to flow into her. The house was full of chaos and we were all calling out to Jesus to bring Samantha back. After a few seconds of this, Samantha shook and started breathing again. I lay her down and by that time the paramedics had arrived and started to take care of her.

Our journey was a very intense one with tests, treatments and just the pain of having your daughter being poked and not understanding what was going on. This was a very trying ordeal on everyone, especially Samantha and Melissa, and it lasted for four days in ICU. It turned out that she had a bad infection of E. coli. Her fever spiked and the enemy was trying to take my daughter.

While she was in the hospital recovering and getting the medicine she needed Melissa and I would decree and declare life, healing and God's plan into her as we sat by the bed. We would sing, worship and decree for hours saturating the room with God's heart.

Praise God that was over two months ago, at the time of this writing, and Samantha is well, very well! Not just that, but she went to Heaven while she was in the hospital and told us about Jesus giving her jewels in a park. She also was near rainbows because she began to tell us about them while she was starting to wake up in the hospital room.

I am telling you this because everyday we pray in our home. Well, most everyday. Wow! The day after Samantha came home was an awesome day of prayer with tears, thanksgiving and loud raucous praise. While I was worshiping and blessing the Lord for what He had done, He said "You think that you have been decreeing and declaring for greater revelation and a greater relationship with Me. I also had you start doing this a year ago so that on September 8th, 2013 you would have enough faith and decrees in you to speak the very life that you had spoken into the atmosphere into your daughter Samantha." I started weeping and started thanking God for His preparation for victory.

This book is not just about reading out loud God's promises but it is an instilling of His life and promise in us so deep that when we face a challenge or trial, the first thing that comes out of our mouths are the decrees, declarations and promises that is His heart in us. This book, *Decree Your Today*, is filled with life - His Life!

PREFACE

In this book you will find thirty-eight thousand, seven hundred and seventeen words of decrees, declarations, Scriptures and heavenly insights of power *that will change your life forever.* You will read about a very special revelation of a number that has probably never entered into your head – that number being 7,500000000000000000. Oh, that is seven quintillion, five hundred quadrillion! What!! WOW!!

The Bible says *How precious are Your thoughts to me, O God! How great is the sum of them! If I should count them, they would be more in number than the sand (on the beach)* (Psalm 139:17-18).

According to the University of Hawaii's research there are seven quintillion five quadrillion grains of sand on all the beaches of the world. That's a 75 with 17 zeros following! "75 with 17 zeros following" (7.5x10^18) is seven quintillion, five hundred quadrillion. That is a crazy number!

Talk about crazy! I am not a math wiz but that number had never entered into my feeble mind until I did some research. I still cannot use any other word other than WOW to describe this. That is just crazy, mind blowing, hard to fathom and hard to believe that anyone could love us like that and think only good thoughts. Yet that is what God thinks about all of us and it always is increasing.

Does God love us? Does He think about us? All the time! His thoughts toward us are more in number than the sand on the seashore or the stars in the sky. What kind of thoughts are they? David says they are precious.

He remembers us graciously and with kindness. The Lord tells us Himself not just the quantity of thoughts He has towards us but the quality of them in Jeremiah 29:11:

For I know the thoughts that I think toward you, says the Lord, thoughts of peace (wholeness, well being, health, blessing) *and not of evil, to give you a future and a hope.*

His thoughts toward us are greater, higher and more glorious than we can ever comprehend. God says through Isaiah, *For My thoughts are not your thoughts, neither are your ways like My ways, says the Lord. For as the heavens are higher than the earth so are My ways higher than your ways and My thoughts higher than your thoughts.* They are glorious, exalted and wonderful. God has wonderful things in store for us.

We need to remember that when we become restless and discouraged waiting for God to come through for us. How absolutely special and incredibly loved we are at those times when we think He has forgotten us. *He can't do it!!*

He is constantly thinking about all five-plus billion people there are on the planet as individuals. He knows exactly how many hairs are on our heads. He knows exactly what we're going through. He knows everything about us.

It's impossible for God to forget you. When the nails were being driven into His hands on the cross, your name was being engraved on them! Don't ever think He's forgotten about you.

As you decree you will begin to hear these awesome and precious thoughts God has for you. As you set your mind on things above you will be changed. You will never find yourself ever doubting that God loves you and that His thoughts toward you are precious, kind, and always increasing in goodness. He has already made decrees for your life. Now, let's decree and establish who He is to the world and re-image Him as a kind, gracious and loving God!

Remember, *God's Word does not return void and He watches over His Word to perform it* (see Isaiah 55:11 and Jeremiah 1:120. In other words, it is His job to bring it to pass and your job to release the Word into your life by declaring, decreeing and proclaiming.

The Word's power is not based on how we feel, think, or anything else, because it is living and endued with inherent power by God. What a freeing principle this is, knowing we could never, ever do it *"right enough!"* All we have to do is speak it, decree it, declare it, announce it and He performs it.

INTRODUCTION

Everyday our mind wakes up to the thought, *"what do I need and want for today?"* Sometimes our needs are so many we can hardly even concentrate. We begin to think, "how am I going to get out of this mess, or what am I going to do about my problems?" Well I have some really good news; you are not alone. God has given us some tools to help us *start our day* by speaking, commanding and bringing Heaven to earth!

These prayers and decrees have been assimilated over a period of about twenty years. Some I have been speaking for many years and others are new ones. No matter, I have put this together to help you change your first thought of the day from your needs to what Heaven wants, and how can you establish and speak on behalf of God and bring His will to my life and the earth.

What is a Decree?

Webster's Dictionary states that de·cree [dih-kree]:

noun

a formal and authoritative order, especially one having the force of law: a presidential decree.

Law – a judicial decision or order.

verb, de·creed, de·cree·ing.

Theology. One of the eternal purposes of God, by which events are foreordained. *Verb* (used with object), verb (used without object) to command, ordain, or decide by decree

We are simply issuing a decree, legislating with an authority given to us by God Himself to bring about His *already stated* divine will.

Divine Will is to make an official order, pronouncement, or legal ruling to effect something. When we speak His word which is *already established in the Heavens*, we enforce it through verbal agreement. Our words become the bridge linking Heaven and earth. Literally speaking, we bring Heaven to earth and when Heaven is loosed, in lives or in the earth at large, things have to change.

To proclaim is to announce something publicly or formally.

You have to speak in order to announce something and to what public do we announce? In the case of spiritual decrees based on the Word we are announcing to evil forces in high places, saying, *God's word has preeminence over what we see in the natural and demand it acquiesce to the spoken living Word.*

To declare is to begin a fierce campaign to get rid of something or start fighting in earnest for or against something.

The word *fierce* should get our attention. We are informed that *the Kingdom of Heaven suffers violence and the violent take it by force* (Matt 11:12). Other words for *fierce* are: violent, ferocious, brutal, vicious, and aggressive, like the anger of a guard dog and with intensity. When we declare over another life the heart and Word of God we are like a guard dog on their behalf. In the case of declaring against injustice there are to be no holds barred in our brutal and vicious assault on the enemy.

Our decrees by our voice are Romans 4:17 in action, *calling those things that are not as though they are;* when you look at a situation and see that it is not the way God intended it to be.

God showed me that when you bless someone, something or a situation, you are actually speaking the original intent that God has for that person, situation or thing. So bless and do not curse! There is "way more" power in blessing!

God said *decree a thing so that it might be established.* That word establish means making it a common occurrence. That is why decreeing and declaring never ever stop. It is going on in the

18

throne room right now. According to Revelation 4, it never stops. They are saying around the throne, *"Holy, holy, holy who was and is to come"* and they bless His name continually. You see my decrees are like praise but they are more than that. They are directed at not just praising but also establishing Heaven on earth.

Let me give you an awesome revelation God showed me about the constant praise in and around the throne. The Lord showed me that the reason that worship and praise never stop is because God is always revealing another part of who He is. His character and His nature are another level of His mercy and love.

One of the ways God showed how this happens is by the living creatures. Once while I was leading worship I was immediately caught up to Heaven and saw the living creatures. *Around and about the throne were four and twenty elders sitting, clothed in white garments; and on their heads, crowns of gold. Out of the throne proceeded lightnings and thunderings and voices* (Revelation 4:4-5a).

What an awesome sight it is! *And there were seven lamps of fire burning before the throne, which are the seven spirits of God. And before the throne there was a sea of glass like unto crystal. And in the midst of the throne, and round about the throne were four living creatures full of eyes before and behind…And the four living creatures each had six wings about him; and they were full of eyes within: and they rest not day and night, saying, 'Holy, holy, holy, Lord God Almighty, which was, and is, and is to come.' And when those beasts give glory and honor and thanks to Him that sat on the throne, who liveth for ever and ever, the four and twenty elders fall down…* (vv. 5-10).

Now that we have this image in our head the Word says they have eyes within and eyes with out. Now imagine these eyes like a mirror ball. Depending on which way you see the mirror ball will determine how you see its reflection.

This is what God showed me. When one of the living creatures wings moved, the reflection just showed another part of God. It could have even been shown in the past but since God is always revealing who and what He is and the incredible vastness of all He is, we have another reason to fall down to give Him honor and glory, worship Him and once again cry Holy, holy, holy!

Wow, just stop right now and get picture of God revealing Himself to you and give Him glory and honor. This, my friend, is why our decrees never stop. Every time we speak and decree He is revealing more of Himself. Could it be that when we are decreeing, the living creature is revealing another dimension of God in the throne room and that is why we are speaking because we saw it manifesting in our spirit? Wow!!!! When you begin to decree the promises of God, He does and will continually reveal Himself to you.

Seven times in the Book of Revelation, when they see Him on His throne, they fall down before Him. When you and I see Him on the throne, we too, should leave our throne, fall down before Him in everything to have the preeminence. Begin to speak what it is you are seeing and you will have an encounter with Heaven and never be the same again.

And the four living creatures, fall down before Him that sat on the throne, and worship Him that liveth for ever and ever and they throw their crowns before the throne of God and they say, 'Thou art worthy, O Lord, to receive glory and honor and power: for thou hast created all things, and for thy pleasure they are and were created" (vv.10-11).

When you speak His Word He gets pleasure and so do we. When you speak what is going on in Heaven and into the atmosphere you immediately step into the eternal time clock of Heaven. You step out of your earthly realm and your situations and circumstances have now become less important.

These decrees and Scriptures will build your faith and you will not want to merely ask for "stuff." You will fall in love with God even more as you co-create with Him and bring what He wants to the earth on a daily basis.

God said, *decree a thing so that it can be established*. When we decree a thing we are agreeing with what God has already said. When you begin to decree promises, which have been alive and forever in the heart of God, you step out of a needs mind-set and step into establishing what God wants.

Remember He said, *Seek ye first the Kingdom of God*. Our decrees establish His Kingdom and He is looking for sons and daughters to step up and establish what He already has said to change the atmosphere. We are called to do just as He did when He said, *Let there be light*. The Bible says that death and life are in the power of speaking. You choose each day what you will establish by what you say.

This book of decrees, prayers and Scriptures are to help you know what to say and how to say it. This will jump start your day and you will be ahead of your needs once you begin to understand the power of establishing the Kingdom of God by your own words.

After you have read this book I pray that you will fall more in love with God, but not just that you will fall in love, but that you will know beyond a shadow of a doubt that you are called according to His purpose to speak, decree and declare His will. After all, Jesus said, *Our Father who art in Heaven, hallowed be you name, Thy Kingdom come thy will be done, ON EARTH AS IT IS IN Heaven!* *(Matthew 6:9,10)*.

You can do this as often as you want. But let me warn you, when you start doing this a lot you will get hooked on bringing Heaven to the earth by your voice rippling through the atmosphere and echoing off the voice of many waters His plan and purpose. You will find that you cannot wait to get to your spot to start your day bringing Heaven to earth!

When you get up each morning to do this or whenever your time of the day is to pray, God will joyfully interrupt your decrees and speak thoughts such as, *How much money would you like, or what can I do for you today.* This Heavenly peace will flood your heart and soul for whatever it is you are needing. You will *just know* that He has it all under control. You will feel His love and kindness of heart and it will remind your heart that He is Jehovah Jireh, the one who sees our need.

Wow, then you will just fall on your knees and worship Him just because of who He is! Many times while I have been in the midst of my decrees, He touches my heart and I just start worshipping and blessing Him as I just get lost in His love, kindness and mercy.

Another awesome benefit of daily declaration, decrees and prayers, is you will begin to hear His voice like never before. That is because, as you begin to speak and decree what He said, you will also begin to hear what He is saying. Your heart and mind will become finely tuned to the frequency of Heaven and His voice as you speak what He has already told you to say through His word. So the benefits are enumerable and the by product is you're not only establishing the Kingdom, but you become His voice on earth knowing what to say, how and when to say it. You will become like a walking trumpet of Heavenly Glory bringing Heaven's decrees and declaration to the world.

As you speak and decree, you will begin to understand the love of God like never before. You will learn that He has precious thoughts about you that never stop. You will discover the power of words as we speak His words. Many mornings I wake up and I am determined to get through all my declarations and decrees yet find that I can barely get through the first page as His love rolls over my soul and I feel His embrace around me. There is need for more declarations at that point for I was already where I longed to be when I got up, with Him! You will find that everything is subject to change when His presence shows up!

Remember, God's Word does not return void and *He watches over His Word to perform it* Isaiah 55:11 Jeremiah 1:12. In other words, His job to bring it to pass and your job to release the Word into your life by declaring, decreeing and proclaiming. The Word's power is not based on how we feel, think, or anything else, because it is living and is endued with inherent power. What a freeing principle this is and knowing we could never, ever do it right enough. All we have to do is speak it, decree it, declare it, announce it and He performs it.

Chapter 1

DECREE & DECLARE TO ESTABLISH

Job 22:28, *You will also declare a thing and it will be established for you; and light will shine on your ways.* (NASB)

Whatever you declare, trust that it is established.

God gives us the power to declare and decree (life and death are in the power of the tongue; Proverbs 18:21). Institute, confirm, settle, summons, and authorize.

In Peter's epistles we learn that we are a royal priesthood. It speaks of royalty like a king ruling and reigning.

I decree that I am a King and a Priest – Kings make decrees, not pleas. That's why the Bible says, "Where the word of a king is, there is power, *dunamis* power". As a king and priest, your words are backed with divine authority. When you pray you issue commands as a king, and minister to God as a priest. Kings don't beg; they rule with Supreme Authority. Therefore having the awareness and understanding that you're a king and priest unto God will cease all weak prayers from your life. You are a King!

Every word spoken is pregnant with creative power. These decrees give birth to whatever we speak. Whether it be good or bad, life or death. When you speak the Word of God, that Word does not return void.

Let's refer to God in Genesis and how each day of creation we read: and God spoke out what He had seen in His mind. And when He spoke, the earth, all the planets, animal's, and human appeared just as He had seen in His mind's eye. What He spoke came to pass.

Now what about ships? We know they are large and driven by strong intense winds, guided by a very small rudder, whatever the will the captain directs. So also the tongue is a small member yet it boasts of great things.

With our mouth, just like a ship's captain, we set our course. We determine the direction we are to be going and we make adjustments just like the captain does, but we use our mouth.

This is why starting your day each day with your decrees and declarations is so important. It sets the direction and plan for your day.

We cannot be tossed to and fro by our circumstances or our issues that pop up. Imagine a ship headed in one direction at one moment, and then turning in the opposite direction in the next. And it keeps doing that over and over? It goes nowhere. This happens when people start speaking about the good things they are expecting to happen one minute, and then the next half hour are talking about all negative things happening to them that are keeping them from getting there. They are turning their lives in circles.

So no matter what, keep speaking the blessing. Keep the ship, which is your mouth, on the steady course. Line up your mouth – the rudder of your life – with the Word of God. Decree and declare where you are going.

Remember, death and life are in the power of the tongue, and those who love it will eat its fruit. Choose to use your tongue to bring life and not death, to bless and not to curse.

When you bless, blessings will be drawn to you, blessings shall come forth and overtake you. Remember what you sow you will also reap. Let's make some decrees now to get our rudder or mouth working.

DECREES

I decree and declare that I dwell in the secret place of the most High God and dwell under the shadow of the Almighty.

Everything that is misaligned I command to come into divine alignment.

I decree I have the mind of Christ and will therefore seek things above and not beneath.

"I know the plans I have for you," says the Lord. "Great and awesome plans to prosper you and not to harm you, plans to give you a hope and a future."

I decree new cycles of victory that will replace old cycles of failure, poverty, and death in my life.

The sword of the Spirit gives me authority and dominion.

I decree my thoughts will be guided and governed by things that are pure, gracious, beautiful, the Word of God –
not bad things or curses.

Old things have passed away, behold God will do a new thing. All things become new of good report.

I decree life, light and love are breaking through the darkness and I will shine with Heaven's light!

My Decrees establish my destiny as I speak, decree and declare the heart of God.

Chapter 2
MY HEAVENLY NUGGETS & INSIGHTS

Make a decree a promise, a word to the Father to stop speaking death. You are not going through, you are coming out! Decree it! Your response is not "I don't know," our response is "God knows the plans that He has for me, I decree it!" His thoughts are neither our thoughts nor our ways like His ways. This is the same God that spoke the whole world into existence.

I approach His throne trembling and shaking, and as I approach His throne of grace, I hear Him say breakthrough is knocking on my window. Breakthrough is rattling my door. Breakthrough is chasing me and breakthrough is following me. Breakthrough is catching me today. Breakthrough is happening all around me. I am breakthrough!

Jesus didn't come to make us religious or for us to live a religion, rather He came to give us life. "I have come that they may have life, and that they may have it more abundantly." (Jn. 10:10) Life comes from relationship and not just by reading books. The Word of God is meant to open to us the person of Jesus Christ by way of Holy Spirit, that we might begin to fellowship with Him in those areas. We are changed from glory to glory. (2 Cor. 3:18) As we behold Him, long for and live and abide in His presence in all of who He is, we begin to be changed into that same image. It is as we are changed that we can behold Him in greater realms of glory, until we come into His fullness. God wants us to fellowship with Him on His level. That level knows that we are seated with Him in Heavenly places and blessed with *every spiritual blessing*!

I am one of God's beautiful creations, created in His image and after His likeness, which is His authority and His power. I am redeemed through the Blood of Jesus and forgiven of all my sins according to the riches of His grace. I am born of the Spirit of God and I am filled with His Holy Spirit. I therefore possess and walk in the fruit of the spirit of love, joy, peace, longsuffering, gentleness, goodness, faith, meekness and temperance. I am an Ambassador for Christ. I am His representative here on earth. I am God's official Legislature and law enforcement agent because I hear the voice from the Holy One.

I am raised with Christ and seek those things that are above that I may please Him. I sit in heavenly places in Him because I dwell in Him and He in me. I remain in the secret place in Him and I abide under the shadow of His wings. I have Kingdom diplomatic immunity against all evil according to Psalm 91 and I now apply God's Word to my life, my family's life and all that is mine.

Therefore, greater is Jesus Christ who lives, rules, reigns, dwells within me and empowers me, than the enemy that is against me in the world. I am victorious, and I walk in total and complete victory in every area of my life. Jesus is seated in heavenly places with all things under His feet. I am hid in Him and therefore demonic principalities, power, ruler of the darkness of this world and spiritual wickedness are also under my feet. I am strong in the Lord and I overcome the wicked one, because the Word of God abides within me.

I am royalty because my Father is King of kings and Lord of lords. I have His royal Blood flowing through my veins and I also have His royal DNA. I am an heir with God. I am joint heir with His Son Jesus Christ. I suffer no lack because He owns everything seen and unseen. Every beast of the forest, the cattle upon a thousand hills, the earth and the fullness thereof, the world and all that is in it belongs to Him. All good things have I inherited through my life in Christ. Every place that the sole of my feet shall tread on

He has already given to me. My first priority and passion in life is to seek first the Kingdom of God and all His righteousness - as a result of my heart and passion to please Him, He causes all my needs and desires to be added unto me.

Is what you are speaking something that God can establish? Do a mouth check. What are you talking about? Let every word spoken be a decree that God can establish according to His word. We can decree it and it is established.

Matthew 18:18; "Verily I say unto you, whatsoever ye shall bind on earth shall be bound in Heaven: and whatsoever ye shall loose on earth shall be loosed in Heaven" (KJV). The word bind means to declare unlawful. The word loose means to declare lawful. How do we bind and loose? Through our declarations!! We declare with our mouths!! Be convinced that you are going to get it. Then declare with authority that you have it! Yea and Amen!

Call on the name of Jesus! He has made us more than conquerors, more than victorious! Behold, He is doing a new thing, shall ye not know it! We are blessed and highly favored. It is the Lord that can shut a door that no man can open and open a door that no man can shut. Decree that thing in your new territory—favor, latter rain. Harvest time is coming-thank You Lord!

Chapter 3
LET US DECREE
A THING

According to James 3:4-5, *Behold also the ships, which though they be so great, and are driven of fierce winds, yet are they turned about with a very small helm, whithersoever the governor listeth. Even so the tongue is a little member, and boasteth great things. Behold, how great a matter a little fire kindleth!*

Because of this word, let's use our tongue to direct the course of our day and make these faith declarations boldly with our mouth – calling things that are not as if they are!

Now you can read quietly but I encourage you to read it out loud. You will find that your physiology will be involved, then your emotions will get involved and God will begin to use you in a powerful way.

Here are some Faith declarations to get your motor started.

TODAY-FAITH DECLARATIONS

I am grateful for today; this is a good day, this is a fantastic day, this is a prosperous day, a wonderful day. This is a glorious day, this is a marvelous day, this is the day the Lord has made I will rejoice and be glad in it.

I have choices to make today. I could be sad, mad, or glad. I choose to be glad.

I am the head and not the tail. I am going over and I'm not going under. God did not bring me this far to let me down or let me drown; I am going to the other side. God will finish what He started in me.

I am a strong finisher. I know how to blow the charge but I do not know how to blow the retreat.

God is setting me up with divine appointments and divine connections.

I will not worry or fret., God has a good plan for my life and family.

I declare that all is well in my family, health, job, business, ministries, and finances; my confidence is in my God! Thank You, God, for today.

I ask You, God, to impart Your heart in me. I ask for supernatural favor, supernatural finances and power in my life today.

I proclaim, The LORD, The LORD God, merciful and gracious, longsuffering, and abundant in goodness and truth.

Move me out of my limits and boundaries.

Lord, use me, give me more ministry with miracles signs and wonders following.

I am totally dependent on the strong hand of God.

2 Chronicles 16:9, *For the eyes of the LORD run to and fro throughout the whole earth, to show himself strong in the behalf of them whose heart is perfect toward him.*

TODAY

The following declarations are to get you going even before you start commanding your day. These words and decrees will lift your faith and you will be in a greater place of strength as you start to command your day!

I thank You, God, for today and that You gave me this day, for this is the only day that I have.

I will live it to the fullest with joy today.

I thank You, God, for Your life flowing in me today.

I thank You, God, for Your presence in my life today.

I thank You, God, for opportunities to share the love of God today.

I praise You, God, for who You are today.

I stir up the gifts of God and ask You to stir them up in me today.

I thank You for the word of wisdom, the word of knowledge manifesting, the gift of faith, the working of miracles and the gifts of healing flowing in me today.

Now I decree that I walk as a man/woman of God today.

I ask and faithfully expect God's blessings for me with signs, miracles and wonders today.

I plead and ask for more territory and more influence to manifest in my life today.

I lean confidently upon the Holy Spirit to guide my thoughts words and actions today.

Let the life and words that I speak attract Heaven today.

I ask You, God, to keep evil far from me as well as any look of impropriety today.

I reach boldly for more than I ever thought You could do in my life today.

I choose to be glad this day and I will remember that God will finish what He started in me.

God is setting me up today for divine appointments and connections.

Father, help me to love righteousness and hate iniquity today!

Now sing a Praise song to our God and start your day praising Him! Take a moment to bless the Lord; thank God for all His benefits and then worship. Tell Him how much you love Him and need Him.

Chapter 4
DECREES FOR WISDOM

And it will be established for you and the light shall shine on your ways (Job 22:28)

I declare and decree that Jesus Christ has been made wisdom unto me. Because I invited the Spirit of Christ's wisdom to fill me to overflowing, I am enriched in all things. The Spirit of Wisdom fills my mind, heart, soul and body. The Spirit of Wisdom empowers me and gives me understanding.

I declare and decree that the fruit of my mouth is righteous and blessing. Wisdom watches over and guards the words that I speak. Wisdom produces creative words within me that bring forth truth, life and edification. Through wisdom, I call forth those things that are not as though they are. With the power of Christ's wisdom I command mountains to be removed. Like my Heavenly Father, I create with my words. Like Him, I say, *"Let there be light"* and light and life and blessings are made manifest.

I declare and decree that I fear God with all my heart, mind and strength because of wisdom's instruction. I grow in the fear of the Lord and therefore receive insight into His secrets and mysteries. The fear of the Lord is clean, enduring forever; therefore I am filled with His purity. The angels of the Lord encamp around me because I fear the Lord. Angelic protection is fortified and increased in my life.

I declare and decree in Jesus' name that I am blessed with the favor of the Lord. His favor is a shield and protection around me. I grow in favor everyday with God and man. I am favored in everything I put my hands to and everywhere I go. The blessing of the Lord's favor opens doors for me that no one can shut. I am blessed beyond measure because of the undeserved and unmerited favor of the Lord.

I declare and decree that Jesus came that I would have life and have it more abundantly. I have a full and abundant life in Him. The Father has chosen gladly to give me His Kingdom, and all the blessings and promises in the Kingdom are mine in Christ Jesus. Every spiritual blessing in the Heavenly places are mine. My life is great in Christ, for He has given me everything that pertains to life and to godliness. He has given me His great, precious and magnificent promises so that by them I can partake of the Divine nature.

I declare and decree that I love wisdom and therefore I am granted the wealth that is in her left hand. My God has given me the power to make wealth in order to establish His covenant. The blessing of wealth comes upon me and overtakes me. I am blessed with prosperity in all that I put my hands to. I am fruitful and I multiply. Goodness and mercy follow me all the days of my life. I sow into good ground and reap 30-60-100 fold return and am increased 1,000 fold more than I am now.

Chapter 5

QUICK START DECLARATIONS FOR TODAY

Read These Declarations and Decrees out loud daily as your prayer to the Lord regarding all the many areas of your life. Why? Romans 10:17 says, *'Faith comes by hearing, and hearing by the Word of God.* SO if faith comes by hearing, that means you have to hear something to increase your faith. If you just read them silently you can't hear what you're reading. Faith comes by hearing! Read out loud!

START YOUR DAY WITH GOD

This is the day that the Lord has made and I will rejoice and be glad in it!

Let everything that has breath praise the Lord! For I will bless the Lord at all times, His Praise shall continually be in my mouth. God's mercy and grace are new and fresh every morning.

I rejoice today because I am a Blood-bought child of God and I have been filled with the Holy Spirit. The Holy Spirit lives in me and is with me wherever I go.

Greater is He that is in me than he that is in the world. The Holy Spirit is bigger than any problem, obstacle, or challenge that I will face. The Holy Spirit will give me wisdom and discernment regarding every decision I need to make today.

When I acknowledge God through prayer and worship, my steps and stops are ordered and directed by the Lord. The Lord gives me wisdom and insight concerning all the affairs of my life. I choose to be a blessing to all those around me.

No matter what happens today, I know God will see me through. I can do all things through Christ Jesus who strengthens me, and if God is for me then no one can be against me.

I choose to honor God today by the words I speak; I will honor God by my actions and attitude. I will honor God by allowing His love, light and truth to shine through me.

I am the head and not the tail; I am above and not beneath. I am blessed coming in and blessed going out.

I am ready for anything and equal to anything through Christ Jesus. He always causes me to triumph. No weapon that is formed against me can prosper. I am strong in the Lord and in the power of His might. Today is going to be a great day!

Now here are the Scriptures which back up the decrees we just made.

This is the day the LORD has made. We will rejoice and be glad in it. Psalms 118:24 (NLT)

I will bless the LORD at all times: his praise shall continually be in my mouth. Psalms 34:1

Let everything that breathes sing praises to the Lord! Praise the Lord. Psalms 150:6

The faithful love of the LORD never ends! His mercies never cease. Great is his faithfulness; his mercies begin afresh each morning. Lamentations 3:22-23 (NLT)

In everything you do, put God first then He will direct your steps and crown all your efforts with success. Proverbs 3:6 (NLT)

I can do all things through Christ who strengthens me. Philippians 4:13

And it shall come to pass, if you shall obey the voice of the LORD your God, to observe and to do all his commandments which I command you this day, that the LORD your God will set you on high above all nations of the earth: And all these blessings shall come on you, and overtake you, if you shall listen and pay attention to the voice of the LORD your God.

Blessed shall you be in the city, and blessed shall you be in the field. Blessed shall be the fruit of your body, and the fruit of your ground, and the fruit of your cattle, the increase of your kine, and the flocks of your sheep.

Blessed shall be your basket and your store. Blessed shall you be when you come in, and blessed shall you be when you go out.
Deuteronomy 28:1-6

No weapon turned against you will succeed. You will silence every voice raised up to accuse you. The servants of the LORD enjoy these benefits; their vindication will come from me. I, the LORD, have spoken! Isaiah 54:17 (NLT)

Chapter 6

NOW!
DECREE YOUR TODAY

Now I stand to command and receive my download from Heaven today. I set my morning and declare it is a new day. Old things have past away, old thoughts, old attacks, old mind sets are gone and all things have become knew!

I take authority over my day in the name of Jesus.

Every element of my day shall cooperate with the purpose and destiny of Heaven.

Today is the dawning of a new day. My season of frustration, failures and lack are over, and I walk in a season of success and prosperity. I say again – old things have passed away; all things have become new.

Today I press toward the mark of the high calling of God in Christ Jesus.

Anything or anyone assigned to undermine, frustrate, hinder, or hurt me, I command to be moved out of my sphere of influence in Jesus's name.

I command my day to fully cooperate with Your plan and purpose for it.

I greet today with great anticipation of the good things You have prepared for me.

I decree and declare that a new day is dawning for my ministry and my job or business, for my finances, for my relationships, and for my health.

I download today success, prosperity, health, wealth, vision, direction, ingenuity, creativity, spirituality, holiness, righteousness, peace, and resourcefulness from Your heart into my day.

I decree and declare that You will be my delight; that Your presence will satisfy me.

I decree and declare that Your word will be my delight.

I decree and declare that my desire will be for Your thoughts and will to reign supreme in me.

I decree and declare that my soul shall prosper in You.

I decree and declare that I will pursue You and Your ways with ALL my heart. I receive Your precious heart for today!

I decree and declare that Your Holy Spirit will lead me.

I decree and declare that I will not satisfy the desires of our sinful nature but instead walk in purity of thoughts, words and deeds.

I decree and declare the fruit of the Holy Spirit will abound in me today.

I decree and declare that I will have ears to hear what the Spirit of the Lord is saying.

I decree and declare that I will be released into a new place of liberty in the spirit.

I decree and declare that I will be set free from all religious yokes and bondages (mindsets).

I decree and declare that I will walk in new levels of accountability in the Truth of God's word.

I decree and declare that I will receive the Spirit of Wisdom and revelation and the eyes of my understanding will be enlightened.

I decree and declare that utterance may be given, that I will open my mouth boldly to make known the mystery of the gospel.

I decree and declare Apostolic boldness. The righteous are as bold as a Lion.

I decree and declare the way of the Lord to be prepared; a spiritual highway will be made for our God; that all obstacles will be removed; God's Glory will be revealed and that all flesh will see it together.

I decree and declare that I will be shifted to new levels of healing and all people will be healed from all manner of sickness and disease.

I decree and declare apostolic authority and dominion in the region where I live; God has set us over the nations and kingdoms to root out, pull down, and destroy, to throw down, and to build and to plant.

I decree and declare every place the soles of our feet shall tread upon, God has given it to us.

I decree and declare that God is a wall of fire around me and He is the glory and the lifter of my head.

I decree and declare a manifestation of the Spirit will flow strong through us without any hindrances: faith, miracles, gifts of healing, prophecy, word of wisdom, word of knowledge, strong discerning of spirits, diverse kinds of tongues, and interpretations of tongues.

I decree and declare that the Anointing and gifts of the Holy Spirit will be revealed to me and abound today.

I decree and declare the spirit of repentance rests on me.

I decree and declare that I shall tell the story of how You've changed my life with others so that they too may come to know You and be satisfied by Your heart of love and forgiveness.

I have a fresh excitement, a fresh mind, a fresh zeal and a fresh anointing for today.

This is the day the Lord has made. It is going to be a Good day!

Chapter 7

PROPHETIC DOWNLOADS, REVELATIONS, MEDITATIONS & POWER DECREES

The beauty and fragrance of the Lord surrounds me and He is glory in the midst of me. The glory of His presence goes before me at all times and gives me rest. His glory is manifest in me. He is goodness that visits my life each day. I decree, "The Lord is good and His lovingkindness endures forever! The Lord is good and His lovingkindness endures forever!"

I decree and declare that God has a good plan for me and it is unfolding before my eyes. I decree that the power and the presence of God goes before me. I decree that the winds of the Holy Spirit blow me to where I am destined to be. I decree that my mouth may speak only good things and the goodness of God. I decree that my Heart will reflect Heaven in all I do and say today. This is my decree today!

Whatever God has spoken into your life, don't let go of it. Keep your vision clear and continue to believe. Nothing is impossible with

God. Nothing can stop us from receiving all God has promised us except our doubt and unbelief. Yes, I'm pregnant -- pregnant with renewed revelation, vision, faith, hope, and promise. You can be, too. Stir up the gift, the calling, the destiny and ask to God to breathe on it once again! Speak to yourself what God said you are and what God called you to be. Encourage yourself by speaking what He thinks about you to yourself!

I confess, declare, decree, shout, announce, shatter the atmosphere with my voice that I am Blessed, everything I touch is blessed, every part of my family is blessed, I am highly favored, I am blessed with every spiritual blessing and ride upon the wings of heavenly glory today in Jesus' name.

Nobody can do what you were born to do better than you. You were born to do what is in your heart. Keep pursuing everything that God has put in your heart to do. Remember the very thing in your heart is what God will use for your comeback! Even Joseph while in prison was using his gift! So never quit being who you are no matter where you find yourself and always remember we are being conformed into His image every second of every day!

God showed me about a year ago that when you bless something or someone, you are actually pronouncing the original intent God had for that person or situation. So when you bless with your heart, your mouth engages the Heavenly realm to go to work to change the situation that you are blessing.

I just heard the Lord say, "Do you want an increase in your anointing"? I answered yes. He said, "Do Acts 10:38: *How God anointed Jesus of Nazareth with the Holy Ghost and with power: who went about doing good, and healing all that were oppressed of the devil; for God was with him.*

The anointing comes by going out and doing good, meeting the needs of people. Ask God to set you up to meet a need! Let's follow the pattern from Jesus and let's see what will happen! Doing good is one thing we can all do! It is inside of us to do good! Be blessed.

Here is a word to encourage someone in transition. Change is never easy and transition without knowledge requires a higher level of patience that is not understandable from the flesh and can only be found and lived in the spirit. Seek those things which are above is your answer. Worship and praise your way through!

Father, cause me to know Your heart, to hear Your voice, to see Your beauty and feel Your loving kindness like a canopy over my life as I start this day! Today is a GREAT day!

This morning my decrees and declarations cannot keep up with the praises that surround You, God, and Your throne. Your heart keeps expanding as I try to keep up with the vastness of Your GREATNESS! Your life today in me is such a declaration of love and I thank You for this day. YOU ARE THE GREAT I AM!

If you feel like a bench warmer in the Kingdom of God, never lose heart; believe and be ready when God calls your name. God told Reinhard Bonnke that He had asked two other people before He called Reinhard's name. Wow! Look what God has done and still does till this day through him. So renew your strength each day by doing all you are supposed to do. Keep your dream alive before you. Be willing to live your call in private where only God sees. That is where our true heart and motives are revealed and made right. But always be ready and remember you are on God's lineup card so be encouraged. Always be ready!!!

When we decree, bless and announce God's agenda each day, we actually swallow up the negative words and worldly vibe that may be present. So change your atmosphere and surroundings!! Fill it with Heaven's vibe and sing the song of the redeemed.

One day we will turn the TV on and the broadcast will say, "Breaking stories all around ...Miracles have broken out all over the US ...we are getting reports of people walking out of ICU wards and an entire school for the blind was reporting that instantly they all could see. Rival gangs getting ready to kill each other just laid their weapons down and fell on there knees and started asking for forgiveness. Prisons report angelic visitations and reconciliation between races. WOWWWWWWWW! We are barely able to cover all that is happening. Wait a minute – this just in: A report of a man who was killed in a car wreck just a few hours ago has suddenly gotten up and left the morgue. WOWWWWWWWW!" Yes, yes, yes! God says, "DECREE and declare, pray, and speak, and my answer is I'll answer THAT prayer. Yes, I'll give you boldness! ' God says, 'I will give miracle working faith. Keep pressing in and believe. Wait you will see more healings! You want signs and wonders? You'll get signs and wonders! LET IT HAPPEN TODAY!!!!

Whatever God has spoken into your life, don't let go of it. Keep your vision clear and continue to believe. Nothing is impossible with God. Nothing can stop us from receiving all God has promised us except our doubt and unbelief.

Yes, I'm pregnant -- pregnant with renewed revelation, vision, faith, hope, and promise. You can be, too.

If you can keep the right attitude when no door is opening, your hallway time can be the door that opens up all doors and possibilities ...keep worshiping in the hallway.

I commit my goals and dreams, my moments, my children, my

wife, my business and my desires to You, oh God. I commit all that I have and are to You. I Surrender it all. God, my life is Yours today. You control all things and I want You to control me. Move me. Mold me in Your ways.

Let my life bring YOU glory and honor, and may I carry the essence and the fragrance of Heaven. Let my words, my actions, my motives, and my desires be Yours. I bow my life and surrender to You. Lord, use me."

God I want to know You in the inward parts of my soul. I want my marrow and my DNA to reflect Your touch on my life. I ask You, God, to fill every area with a fire that comes from Your heart. I want to know You more than just as a minister or even a Christian. I want to know You as a Father. I want Your heart to beat in mine so that if compromise comes knocking at my door it is met with Your heartbeat – the beat of obedience and surrender; not my way but Your way Yahweh. Lord, fill me with Your light life and love this day. I want to reflect Your Glory and re-image You to the world, like the God who You ARE – slow to anger, merciful, kind and loving. God, I am Yours!!!

You cannot do anything without Revelation. Revelation is the birthing chamber of the unseen... things which have not been created. Open our eyes, God, to first see You. Then as we see You, Revelation flows and the unseen begins to be seen.

I release the anointing and the lightning power of God upon your life today. I speak those things that are not as though they are in your life. I speak God's divine entrance and encounter into every situation, circumstance and condition facing you. If you are at ZERO, you are at a place where God'z creative force of HIS LIGHT, LIFE AND LOVE will begin to flow. Release the anointing into everything you speak, touch, read or send and watch what God will do for you.

God is calling us to be spiritual scientists; a scientist while doing his experiments gains experience. This is how the initiatives of Heaven work; as we learn how to hear God's voice we are experimenting on obeying and trusting God. Then each time we experiment we see success; we gain experience which equals BOLDNESS. Then we have influence in the world. The world needs a Godly encounter from people who know His heart!

Chapter 8
LIFE OR DEATH[1]

MIRACLE IN YOUR MOUTH

There are those within the Body of Christ that have a misunderstanding when it comes to faith and healing. I have heard some say that those being attacked with sickness or disease should deny that it even exists, and to mention it at all would be a serious breach in the workings of productive faith. The Bible tells us in John 4:23 that the true worshipers of God worship in spirit and in truth. If we are going to get the results we see in the promises of the Word of God, we need to make sure we are operating in truth.

While we do not deny that sickness or disease is attacking our bodies, if we've been diagnosed with such a condition, we do recognize that we have the God-given right to deny sickness or disease a place within our bodies based upon the authority of our Covenant Promises. I call that living in the "Heavenly reality"; kind of like when Jesus said, "The girl is asleep."

After all, 1 Corinthians 6:19 reminds us that our body is the temple of the Holy Spirit. A person must come to the understanding that, through the established Word of God, the right of healing has been declared to us and is a part of the package of salvation that was purchased for us at the cross through the shed Blood of the Lord Jesus Christ.

We need to understand that effective faith must be active and functioning within two separate areas of our being, which is more

---

[1] Compiled in part from material by Dan Downey www.savedhealed.com used by permission.

than believing only within our heart. In fact, the Scripture tells us that faith is a true action word. James 2:26 states; *"For as the body without the spirit is dead, so faith without works is dead also"* (KJV). True faith requires action. I am not talking about a "works trip." However, we must realize that real biblical faith, the kind that brings results, is proactive and assertive.

Take a look at Romans 10:6-11: *"The word is near you, in your mouth and in your heart"* (that is, the word of faith which we preach): *that if you confess with your mouth the Lord Jesus and believe in your heart that God has raised Him from the dead, you will be saved. For with the heart one believes unto righteousness, and with the mouth confession is made unto salvation"* (KJV 2000). It's very clear to see that when appropriating faith, we need to have it functioning and working together harmoniously in both places, in our mouth and in our heart.

Many think this block of Scripture is speaking only of salvation leading to eternal life. However, when you do a word study on this word "salvation" you find this word speaks just as strongly of physical and emotional healing in the present as it does of eternal life. And why shouldn't it? That's exactly how Jesus used this word when He walked the earth, both for physical healing and for the forgiveness of sin. Do you see it? "For with the heart one believes unto righteousness (being right or whole), and with the mouth confession is made unto salvation/healing."

We need the heart (believing, being fully convinced with a knowing faith) and the mouth (speaking out, declaring the truth of what the Word reveals to us) working together. Generally, either one used alone will not bring about the desired results. We must employ the fullness of what the Word is telling us IF we want to realize the fullness of the promised blessing.

The Bible has much to say about the important role our words play in our lives, and all the more when we are speaking the Word of God over our situation. No, it's not mind over matter – it's God's

Word over the matter! And His Word is truth (John 17:17. Yes), it may be a natural, medical fact that sickness or disease is attacking your body, but the TRUTH says *"by His stripes you were healed "*- 1 Peter 2:24. His truth supersedes natural fact! This again is what I call "Heaven's reality".

We need to learn not to focus on the problem but instead to focus on the answer. Continually speaking out how bad things are will not bring about relief. That's only a declaration of what is happening to you and not a declaration of the reality of what's been given to you – your position of righteousness in Him. Speaking out your possession of the Word of God will bring about the desired change! It's an exchange of the natural for the supernatural – His life, the abundant life, that which has been given to us as a free gift (John 1:12).

Now a WARNING: By reading the words below you may have to retrain yourself regarding how you speak. However, the results will be simply heavenly!

Ephesians 6:17, *And take the helmet of salvation, and the sword of the Spirit, which is the word of God.*

NOTE: The Greek word for "word" here is "rhema" which means the spoken word. The Word of God is a sword when it comes out of your mouth. See Revelation 19:15 – you see the sword coming out of the mouth of Jesus – the spoken Word. Speak the Word over your situation until you have what the Word says and it will activate the angels on your behalf!

James 3:6 , *And the tongue is a fire, a world of iniquity. The tongue is set among our members as that it defiles the whole body, and sets on fire the course of nature; and it is set on fire by hell.*

NOTE: Since this is true, then the reverse of this fact is also true. If the tongue has the ability to defile and tear down, then with the tongue we can also bless and build up and receive the benefit of that blessing by the Word of God.

Mark 11:23, *For assuredly, I say to you, whoever says to this mountain, 'Be removed and be cast into the sea,' and does not doubt in his heart, but believes that those things he says will come to pass, he will have whatever he says.*

NOTE: Did you notice that in this Scripture Jesus only mentions "believe" one time but mentions "say" three times? Read the context of this Scripture in Mark 11 and you will clearly see Jesus was talking about faith of the heart and a person's words working together – and He was speaking to a fig tree! We see that words are a vehicle of releasing our faith. Speak to your "mountain" or obstacle and command it to be removed - you are way more important than an old fig tree! How much more will it work for you!!!

Job 22:28, *You will also declare (or decree) a thing, and it will be established for you; so light will shine on your ways.*

NOTE: Will you dare to take God at His Word and lay claim to the Covenant Promises of health and boldly declare to the devil and hell that you will not be held down by your present situation, but will instead have the reality of the blessing of health established within you? Say it out loud if you believe it – "I will have health – I refuse and negate this sickness to stay within me – By His stripes I am and I was healed – it's mine and I will not be denied, I say by faith that I have it now!!!" One of the most powerful things you can do is to set your will in line with the Word of God.

Isaiah 57:19, *I create the fruit of the lips: Peace, peace to him who is far off and to him who is near," Says the LORD, "And I will heal him.*

NOTE: The Lord is clearly speaking here and look what He is saying; "I create the "fruit" of the lips. What kind of fruit is proceeding from your mouth? Are you giving the Lord words (substance) that He can work with, which is His Word? Or are you only speaking the problem and what the doctors are saying about you? See Isaiah 55:11: He said His Word would not return to Him void. How does it return to Him? When we speak it. This is powerful!!

> Psalm 91:1-2, *He who dwells in the secret place of the Most High Shall abide under the shadow of the Almighty. I will say of the LORD, "He is my refuge and my fortress; My God, in Him I will trust.*

Notice the principle and the important role words play in taking hold of the promises, security and deliverance of God as set forth in this great psalm. In the beginning of this psalm the psalmist speaks out making bold faith declarations, laying claim to His covenant with God through His words. Immediately, in the beginning of your circumstances or trial, get your faith into motion by declaring who God is to and what He has promised to do for you. Look at John 1:1, *In the beginning was the Word.* Make the Word your beginning in every area in life.

Proverbs 10:11, *The mouth of the righteous is a well of life.*

Proverbs 12:6, *The mouth of the upright will deliver them.*

Proverbs 12:14, *A man will be satisfied with good by the fruit of his mouth.*

Proverbs 12:18, *The tongue of the wise promotes health.*

Proverbs 13:3, *He who guards his mouth preserves his life.*

Proverbs 14:3, *The lips of the wise will preserve them.*

Proverbs 15:2, *The tongue of the wise uses knowledge (The Word) rightly, but the mouth of fools pours forth foolishness.*

Proverbs 15:4, *A wholesome tongue is a tree of life, but perverseness in it breaks the spirit.*

NOTE: A wholesome tongue is one that speaks in line with the Word of God.

Proverbs 15:4 (AMP), *A gentle tongue [with it's healing power] is a tree of life, but willful contrariness in it breaks down the spirit.*

Proverbs 16:23, *The heart of the wise teaches his mouth, and adds learning to his lips.*

 NOTE: Discipline yourself to speak the Word over yourself and your situation. Dig in to the Word and find out what the Lord has to say about your condition. Don't rely upon your friends or even your pastor, you need to see it for yourself. Your life is at stake here!

Proverbs 16:24, *Pleasant words are like a honeycomb, sweetness to the soul and health to the bones.*

NOTE: Do you see it? God's Word is pleasant and it will bring health to your body and peace to your soul! See Proverbs 4:20-22 God's Word is life to those that find them and health (lit. medicine) to all their flesh.

Proverbs 18:7, *A fool's mouth is his destruction, and his lips are the snare of his soul.*

NOTE: Chose not to be a fool and neglect retraining yourself to speak the Word instead of the problem. Be wise, watch your words!!!

Proverbs 18:20-21, *A man's stomach shall be satisfied from the fruit of his mouth, from the produce of his lips he shall be filled. Death and life are in the power of the tongue, and those who love it will eat its fruit.*

NOTE: Whose report are you going to believe? The Word here clearly states the you "shall" be filled with the fruit or produce of your mouth – it's a law, it will happen. Know this, you WILL eat the fruit of what you are saying; it's your choice – the effects of life or the effects of death!

Proverbs 21:23, *Whoever guards his mouth and tongue keeps his soul (life) from troubles.*

NOTE: Let's be careful to put a guard on our mouth and say only what the Word says about our situation. (See 2 Corinthians 10:3-5). I know it's tempting to moan and complain, but that won't bring about health. Don't give in!

Proverbs 22:12, *The eyes of the LORD preserve knowledge, but He overthrows the words of the faithless.*

Joshua 1:8, *This Book of the Law (The Word) shall not depart from your mouth, but you shall meditate in it day and night, that you may observe to do according to all that is written in it. For then you will make your way prosperous, and then you will have good success.*

Isaiah 55:11, *So shall My word be that goes forth from My mouth; It shall not return to Me void, but it shall accomplish what I please, and it shall prosper in the thing for which I sent it.*

NOTE: God's Word will not fail when it is believed in the heart and spoken forth in faith – The Lord God says so!

Isaiah 54:17, *"No weapon formed against you shall prosper, and every tongue which rises against you in judgment you shall condemn. This is the heritage of the servants of the LORD, and their righteousness is from Me," Says the LORD.*

NOTE: According to the promise of the Word in Galatians 3:13 and Isaiah 53:5, sickness and disease are illegal in your body and are judging you falsely as still under the curse. Condemn the disease or sickness with the Word of God and command it to leave your body. Do this every time you think about it. Don't ever stop and accept the lie - Persistence breaks down resistance!

Hebrews 11:3, *By faith we understand that the worlds were framed by the word of God, so that the things which are seen were not made of things which are visible.*

NOTE: Here again the Greek word for "word" here is "rhema" which means the spoken word. And of course we see clearly from the Genesis account of creation this is so. He spoke the world in to existence. Ephesians 5:1 tells us to be imitators of God – What kind of world are you framing with your words? What are you establishing when you speak?

After reading through these powerful truths regarding the words of our mouth, you can see why it is so important to lay claim to the Scriptures personally, declaring them in the first person tense, inserting your name in the them where it is applicable and boldly declaring that the promise already belongs to you and you have it now.

This is an almost everyday part of my life. I decree the Heart of God to the world and when I do I am establishing His Kingdom.

So start today to start speaking like this "No weapon formed against me shall prosper, I am free from the law of sin and death and I am under the perfect law of liberty. I am a free man. I'll never be sick another day of my life, I am the healed of the Lord, I am NOT sick. Sickness and disease have no right to live in me, because I am redeemed from the curse of the law. I walk in love, I walk in faith, I walk in health, and the power of God resides in me. I am part of the Body of Christ, therefore I am declared righteous through Him. I am righteous now, and I deny the enemy any place in my life. I will reign in life through Jesus Christ, empowered by His Spirit."

All of these are taken from the truths of the Word of God. As you read through this book, decree, declare and announce the heart of God to the world and your heart will change everyday by decreeing His heart!

Chapter 9

RIGHTEOUS DECREES & VICTORIOUS DECLARATIONS

I decree the Victorious Declaration of Praise even when I don't feel like declaring it:

I praise You for I am wonderfully and powerfully made out of Your image and likeness.

I am called to speak and demonstrate Your heart to the world.

I am a Blood bought, Blood washed child of the highest God, ready to do His bidding on the earth.

You are the most awesome, incredible loving kind father I know. God, help me to walk in all that You are.

God, You are so awesome!

You are magnificent beyond the boundaries of beauty.

Your holiness and matchless power can never be contained! Containment itself would never dare to attempt such an action.

You are the most powerful, holy, righteous, just God!

I have been set free. I am free to love, to worship, to trust, with no fear of rejection or of being hurt.

I operate in all gifts of the Holy Spirit, which are tongues and interpretation of tongues, the working of miracles, discerning of spirits, the word of faith, the word of knowledge, the word of wisdom, healings, and prophecy.

I take every thought captive unto the obedience of Jesus Christ, casting down every imagination, and every high and lofty thing that exalts itself against the knowledge of God.

No weapon that is formed against me shall prosper, but every tongue that rises against me in judgment, I shall show to be in the wrong.

You are powerful. I am reminded of the powerful oceans in all the world that toss huge vessels to and fro and yet these massive waves are in absolute awe of You, the most powerful God.

Better is one day in Your courts than a thousand elsewhere; I would rather be a doorkeeper in the house of my God than dwell in the tents of the wicked.

There is NONE like You – no, not one!

For the Lord God is a sun and shield; the Lord bestows favor and honor; no good thing does He withhold from those whose walk is blameless. Lord Almighty, blessed is the one who trusts in You.

You, God, are my God, earnestly I seek You; I thirst for You, my whole being longs for You, in a dry and parched land where there is no water. I have seen You in the sanctuary and beheld Your power and Your glory.

Because Your love is better than life, my lips will glorify You. I will praise You as long as I live, and in Your name I will lift up my hands. I will be fully satisfied as with the richest of foods; with singing lips my mouth will praise You

You are Holy. I am reminded of the mighty angels that declare who You are moment by moment, shouting, "Holy! Holy! Holy!" The pure power of Who You are which is Holy is uncontainable rushing; revealing Your glory.

The holiness of You, all Consuming Fire, would obliterate our physical bodies to particles of dust...yet You love us with a Love that can not be translated into human action or human words of any sort ...for You are LOVE.

You are righteous. I am reminded of Who You are! The foundation that stands; You are never failing to support, never falling apart; never losing Your sustaining power. The changes

and shifting of time that passes through cannot penetrate You! For You are the Foundation of which I stand because of Jesus Christ.

You are just. I am reminded of Your throne. The foundation of Your throne is righteousness and justice. You are my Advocate and my Standby even though I do not deserve it. You remain my EVER PRESENT help in time of need and trouble!

Hallelujah! Father! You are magnified! You be glorified in my eyes! My eyes must see that which already is, and that is You! You are high and lifted up – higher than anything that tries to come against me. As my mind magnifies you, the out of control thoughts become de-magnified! Submitting to you causes a resistance simultaneously to my screaming flesh that wants to receive depression! You are All Consuming Fire that obliterates, annihilates and melts away the unknowing want and desire to be a victim when You see me as a victor! You are so Awesome God... beyond the boundaries of awesome. You are incredibly God! My mouth cannot keep up with the praises that surround You...for You are The Great I Am!

Chapter 10

DECLARATIONS FOR HEALING[1]

We decree and declare that by Jesus' stripes _____ is already healed. So we command that this day _____ body will line up and function in the way that You, God created it to function. (1 Peter 2:24) We give You praise, Father, for strengthening _____body, soul and spirit.

We need You, Father, and we ask You, Holy Spirit, to come and reveal Your love, Your presence and Your healing power in our lives. You said in Your Word that "mercy triumphs over judgment" (James 2:13).

Heavenly Father, we ask You in the name of Jesus for Your mercy to come now and reveal them; remove any and all judgments in our lives that may be enabling separation with family, friends, community and the body of Christ. Show us all things that may be hindering healing and deliverance, Heavenly Father, as we cry out "deliver us from evil"!

⊹

We bless the LORD, our Jehovah Rophe who forgives all iniquity, heals all disease and redeems every life from destruction!

---

[1] Acknowledgment to pastor Larry Thomas for material in this chapter.

We join our faith in agreement with the Word of God, declaring that whatsoever we bind on earth is bound in Heaven and whatsoever we loose on the earth is loosed in Heaven. We welcome the presence of Jesus, the I AM, in our midst and presence to back and enact the words of this declaration. We bind the power of _____ (etc.) over _____and command every tissue and cell to function as God intends. We loose the anointing of God to remove every burden and utterly destroy the yoke! We demand the name of this disease to bow down and submit itself unto the Name of JESUS, in whom is life, health, healing and salvation!

✦

We speak to the disease named _____ (etc.) and say there is a Name that you must bow to. You will bow to the Name of Jesus. That Name is a Name above every other name. You are commanded to loose your assignment on _____ life. You are commanded to release and leave his/her body now. Every system in his/her body that has been disrupted because of your influence, I call it back into full operation; the blood pressure, the red blood cells, white blood cells, and electrolytes to balance out in the name of Jesus. All fluid that has accumulated in areas of the body that it should not be I speak to you to re-absorb in the name of Jesus. Peristalsis return to his/her intestines immediately, awake and function properly in the name of Jesus. Lord, strengthen every muscle and organ where atrophy has tried to take place in his/her body. (Name the disease), I decree and declare this day that you will die. You have no control over_____ . He/she is loosed from the infirmity of (name disease) and all its future abilities to return (Lk. 13:12).

✦

I speak to every electromagnetic frequency and every chemical frequency in _____ body to come into right alignment with

70

the Living Word of the Most High God. I speak to _____
immune system to awake and arise and to destroy every
rebellious cell in the name of Jesus.

✦

Based on the Word of God, Revelation 12:11, we appropriate the
Blood of the Lamb and declare victory over every established
cancerous cell! We decree the Blood of the Lamb ministers
life and health to the body and command tumors and invasive
growths in the ovaries, pelvis and abdominal cavities to dissipate,
be removed and cast out in the NAME of JESUS.

✦

We further command abnormal genes to cease in their
reproduction. We declare healthy white blood cells will increase
and expertly carry out their created function, removing all
infection, disease and cancerous cells from the body. We thereby
speak to the intestines and command them to wake up and
function the way they were created.

✦

In the power of the Holy Spirit, we take full authority and pull
down every altar of affliction, disease and discomfort that has
been built against_____ body and his/her destiny. We call
forth healing NOW. And we make this decree -that You, Lord,
are the Lord that heals_____ (Exodus 15:26) Thank You for
releasing Your healing power!

✦

We come to You, Lord, this day praying in faith concerning
_____ healing and we know according to Your word
that the prayer of faith shall save_____, and You Lord will
raise_____ up. (James 5:15) So upon this Scripture we
announce that every weapon of fear, infirmity, oppression, and

the power of death be destroyed and terminated by the fire of the God of Elijah, in Jesus' name. Let the rain of Your blessing fall upon him/her and his/her family NOW!

It is written, *"Behold I have given you power to tread on serpents and scorpions, and over all the power of the enemy, and nothing shall in any means harm you."* (Luke 10:19) So, in the Name of Jesus Christ of Nazareth, "the Lord rebuke you, Satan", and the Blood of Jesus is against you and all your set up plans. Go now, go, go now and do not return!

We decree and declare that this day that_____ will bless the Lord, O her soul: and all that is within him/her, she will bless His holy name. From the rising of the sun _____ will bless the Lord, and he/she will not forget all His benefits: but he/she shall know Who forgives all him/her iniquities; and who heals all of her diseases. (Psalm 103:1-3)

We renounce any self-will pride, selfish ambition and lawlessness and anything and everything that is not pleasing to You, God, and ask You to reveal any such thing to us and set us free from it. We ask You, Heavenly Father, to forgive us of past family generations of the sin of pride and self-willed ambition. Forgive them Father, they didn't know what they were doing.

We decree and declare that this day that_____ has diligently hearkened to the voice of You, Lord her God, and he/she has done that which is right in Your sight, and he/she will continue to give ear to Your commandments, and keep all Your statues, So we thank You that You will not put any diseases upon him/her, for You are the Lord that heals him/her (Exodus 15:26).

It is decreed and declared that _____ shall serve You the Lord his/her God, and You shall bless him/her, and You will take sickness away from the midst of him/her. We decree and declare that there shall be nothing cast to him/her young, nor shall he/she be barren and the number of his/her days You God will fulfill. (Exodus 23:25-26)

✦

We call Heaven and earth to record this day against _____ that God has set before_____ life and death, blessing and cursing: therefore we decree and declare that_____ chooses life, that both she/he and his/her seed may live. (Deuteronomy 30:19-20). Therefore every agenda of untimely death in his/her life and the life of his/her family is being dismantled and annulated in the powerful name of Jesus.

✦

In the name of Jesus Christ we bind up the strongman of death, we rebuke the spirit of cancer/or_____, Leviathan, infirmity, fear and every evil thing and loose it and give it no place. We bind up every operation of the spirit of _____ & Leviathan which would steal blood to feed the cancer/or _____ and command every blood vessel supplying blood to the cancer cells or tumors/or_____ to be cut off, shrink, dissolve and be removed NOW in Jesus

✦

This day it is declared from the mountaintop that because _____ hast made the Lord his/her refuge and even the most High his/her habitation; than there shall no evil befall him/her neither shall any plague come near his/her dwelling. Because You, Lord, hath set Your love upon_____, therefore You, Lord, will deliver him/her and You will set him/her on high, because _____has known Your name. We thank You, Lord, that as_____ calls upon You, we believe You will answer him/her.

You will be with _____ in trouble and will deliver him/her, and honor him/her. With long life You will satisfy _____ and show him/her Your salvation. (Psalm 91:9-10, 14-16)

From out of Zion we sound a decree that _____ will not die, but live and declare the works of the Lord his/her God. (Psalm 118:17)

From out of Zion we sound a decree that _____ will not die, but live and declare the works of the Lord his/her God. (Psalm 118:17)

We decree and declare that the law of the Spirit of life in Christ Jesus has made _____ free from the law of sin and death. We thank You that the Spirit of God that raised up Jesus from the dead dwells in_____, and You, God, that raised up Christ from the dead shall also quicken_____ body by Your Spirit that dwells in him/her (Romans 8:2,11).

Acts 20:32 (AMP), *And now [brethren], I commit you to God [I deposit you in His charge, entrusting you to His protection and care]. And I commend you to the Word of His grace [to the commands and counsels and promises of His unmerited favor]. It is able to build you up and to give you [your rightful] inheritance among all God's set-apart ones (those consecrated, purified, and transformed of soul).*

NOTE - Oh, the power of the Word of God! It is designed, ordained, and anointed to build you up, to strengthen and bring healing, stability, wholeness and deliverance. AND it releases your inheritance as a child of God. All of who He is and all of what He has. Don't fret about what is, get into His Word and allow the Word to manifest the Life of God - His Grace - into your moment. As a believer, you're in the Family of God. Expect the Family benefits.

Psalm 119:50, *"This is my comfort in my affliction, for your Word has given my life."*

Romans 10:17,*"So then faith comes by hearing and hearing by the word of God."*

NOTE - Faith for healing comes by hearing God's Word concerning healing. So just as you may be taking medicine two or three times a day, do the same thing with the promises in the Word of God regarding healing, and allow your faith to be built up! You'll be amazed at the change that will take place.

Proverbs 4:20-22, *"My Son, attend to My words; incline thine ear unto My sayings. Let them not depart from thine eyes; keep them in the midst of thine heart. For they are life unto those that find them, and health (Lit. medicine) to all their flesh."*

NOTE - Here it is as plain as it can be: the taking of God's Word is life and medicine to your flesh. So just don't take your prescribed natural medicine alone, add the Word of God along with it. Prescribed medicine can heal and help some things, but God's medicine can heal all.

John 8:32, "And ye shall know the truth, and the truth shall make you free."

NOTE - The Word of God is truth see John 17:17. Once you know the truth concerning healing in God's redemptive plan, then you can begin to exercise faith and expect the promises of God to manifest in you - and they will - REJOICE!!!

Jeremiah 23:29, *"Is not My word like a fire? says the LORD, And like a hammer that breaks the rock in pieces?"*

NOTE - Get this fact down deep into your heart. The Word of God IS an all consuming fire that will melt away and burn off that which is not of God, and a powerful crushing force to break apart even the toughest and most stubborn circumstances. Continue taking the hammer of God's Word and continue to hit the situations in your life that are not of God, until they give way and become exactly as the Word says they should be. Persistence breaks down resistance!

2 Timothy 3:16-17, *All Scripture is given by inspiration of God, and is profitable for doctrine, for reproof, for correction, for instruction in righteousness, that the man of God may be complete, thoroughly equipped for every good work.*

NOTE - Does your body and/or mind need correction? God's Word is just the medicine. According to this verse, we see that it is His will that you may be complete and thoroughly equipped for every good work. If you are sick you cannot fully do the work of the ministry – know that God wants you to be able bodied, a living example in every area of His grace, mercy and power.

John 6:63, *It is the Spirit who gives life; the flesh profits nothing. The words that I speak to you are spirit, and they are life.*

NOTE - God's Word is healing, it will bring health to your flesh. See Proverbs 4:22. That's why it is so important to continue to go over the healing Scriptures daily, therefore building your faith in the area of healing, imparting the very life of God into your cells as well as your mind. Fill up on God's Word!

John 15:7, *If you abide in Me, and My words abide in you, you will ask what you desire, and it shall be done for you.*

Isaiah 55:11, *So shall my word be that goeth forth out of my mouth: it shall not return unto me void, but it shall accomplish that which I please, and it shall prosper in the thing whereto I sent it.*

NOTE - God's Word on healing will accomplish healing in you.

Jeremiah 1:12 (AMP), *I am alert and active watching over My Word to perform it.*

NOTE - God is looking, searching eagerly for someone to take Him at His Word so that He can perform it on their behalf.

Joshua 21:45, *Not a word failed of any good thing which the LORD had spoken to the house of Israel. All came to pass.*

NOTE - How much more sure is this promise to us since our covenant with God is based upon the shed Blood of Jesus Christ!

Leviticus 18: 4-5, *You shall observe My judgments and keep My ordinances, to walk in them: I am the Lord your God. You shall therefore keep My statutes and My judgments, which if a man does, he shall live by them: I am the Lord.*

NOTE - Here we see the importance of walking in obedience to the Word of God, "which if a man does, he shall live by them." The key phrase here is "he shall live" and it's actually just one word in the Hebrew language: *chayay*. This word just doesn't mean to sustain life, barely getting by, but literally means to live prosperously, with vibrancy, being free or revived from sickness, faintness, discouragement, and even death. It carries with it the implied meaning of restoration, revival, and even growth or increase of well-being. If we had to apply a single word to this, it would be to flourish or to thrive in life to its full. Now you can see the true meaning of this passage. If a man applies himself to the Word in obedience, he will flourish in all areas of life and thrive and increase! This not only includes healing and health but all other areas of our life as well, financial, emotional, relational, intellectual, etc.

HEALING IS A GOOD GIFT FROM GOD!

James 1:17, *Every good gift and every perfect gift is from above, and cometh down from the Father of lights, with whom is no variableness, neither shadow of turning.*

NOTE - Healing is a wonderful gift from God, and here again is another proof that He does not change. What He did yesterday He will do again today - Praise the Lord, He is still the Healer!!!

1 Corinthians 3:21-22, *Therefore let no one boast in men. For all things are yours: whether Paul or Apollos or Cephas, or the world or life or death, or things present or things to come--all are yours.*

NOTE - This says it so clear; the Lord is holding nothing back from us. Surely healing is included in the claim of "all things" and certainly is included in the word "life." Begin to praise the Lord for your healing which is a gift to you from the Lord, and the manifestation that will come as you receive the promise by faith.

Romans 11:29, *For the gifts and the calling of God are irrevocable.*

NOTE - He's the giver of gifts and He doesn't take them back, they cannot be canceled out!

Philippians 2:13, *For it is God who works in you both to will and to do for his good pleasure.*

Matthew 11:28 (AMP), *Come to Me, all you who labor and are heavy-laden and overburdened, and I will cause you to rest. [I will ease and relieve and refresh your souls.]*

NOTE - The word 'rest' here literally means to cease from toil or labor in order to recover and collect one's strength, and implies a feeling of wholeness and well being. Place your focus onto Jesus and all that He has purchased for you. Take the focus off of the circumstances, and begin praising Him for all that He has done for you. As a child of God, you are highly favored by God - He's given it all to you. Spend time each day just loving on God. Come to Him through intimate worship, and experience this rest.

Deuteronomy 29:29, *The secret things belong to the Lord our God, but those things which are revealed belong to us and to our children forever, that we may do all the words of this law.*

NOTE - This Scripture makes it so clear that healing and health belong to you and your posterity – your family line. Healing has been revealed to us through the Word of God – declared to us through the shed covenant Blood of Jesus Christ on the cross. Every Scripture on this page is declaring your revealed covenant right. Dig in and take hold of it by faith and refuse to let go of your birthright!!!

Isaiah 33:24, *And the inhabitant will not say, "I am sick"; the people who dwell in it (Zion) will be forgiven their iniquity.*

NOTE - While this chapter in Isaiah is dealing with impending judgment with God's people (Zion) for repentance, notice that the forgiveness of their iniquity also provided for the healing of their bodies. How much more does this apply for us now in this time, having Jesus Christ as our Lord and Savior, who has redeemed us from the curse of the Law being made a curse for us (Galatians

3:13) who by His stripes we were healed (1 Peter 2:24), has made this Scripture a reality to us (spiritual Zion) through His shed Blood on the cross!!!

We Have Been Redeemed Out From Under The Bondage Of Sickness & Disease!

Galatians 3:13-14, *Christ hath redeemed us from the curse of the law, being made a curse for us; for it is written, Cursed is every one that hangs on a tree: That the blessings of Abraham might come on the Gentiles through Jesus Christ.*

NOTE - The curse of the law includes sickness and disease and is found in Deuteronomy 28:15-68. The first 14 verses of the chapter pertain to the blessing, and the rest of the chapter describes the curse! By the shed Blood of Jesus Christ we were purchased out of or out from under the curse!!! Especially look at verse 61, it states: "all sickness and all disease in the world, even those not written in the Book, (is included in the curse)" – so therefore we are redeemed from it all!!!

Proverbs 26:2, *Like a flitting sparrow, like a flying swallow, so a curse without cause shall not alight.*

NOTE - As we continue in Christ, the curse has no right to take root in our lives. Take a firm stand against it, and command its effects to leave in the Name of Jesus! You are a child of the King.

Romans 8:2, *For the law of the Spirit of life in Christ Jesus has made me free from the law of sin and death.* And the effects of death and the curse!

Colossians 1:13, *He has delivered us from the power of darkness and conveyed us into the Kingdom of the Son of His love.*

NOTE - Remember there is no sickness or disease in the Kingdom of God! Here again is another wonderful Scripture proving your birthright of healing.

1 John 3:8b, *For this purpose the Son of God was manifested, that He might destroy the works of the devil.*

Take a look at this same verse in the Amplified version - *The reason the Son of God was made manifest (visible) was to undo (destroy, loosen, and dissolve) the works the devil [has done].*

NOTE - There is no doubt that sickness and disease are works of the devil, introduced to mankind through the fall as part of the curse. This Scripture is very clear that Jesus came to undo the works of the devil. Be assured that He accomplished His task- further proof that sickness and disease have no legal right to remain in your body as a child of God! Command it to go in Jesus' name!

2 Corinthians 3:17, *Now the Lord is the Spirit; and where the Spirit of the Lord is, there is liberty."*

NOTE - If you are born again, if you've asked Jesus to come into your heart, then you are saved, you are a child of God and the Spirit of God dwells within your heart – make no mistake about it!!! Therefore, according to this Scripture, freedom and liberty from bondage in any form belong to you, and you should expect it. It's your covenant right. Receive this personally as the truth that it is for you right now!!! Lift your hands to the Lord and begin to praise Him and worship Him for His goodness to you.

John 8:36, *Therefore if the Son makes you free, you shall be free indeed.*

NOTE - The Greek thought here is not just "free," but undeniably and unquestionably free. The Amplified version reads: *So if the Son liberates you [makes you free men], then you are really and unquestionably free.*

Let this truth of victory soak down deep into your heart and dispel all thoughts of doubt and fear. Praise God, sickness and disease have no right to be in us; they cannot stay, they have to go! Shout it out - "I'm a free man!!!"

Chapter 11

THE COMMA AND THE STANDARD

Isaiah 59:19, *So shall they fear The name of the LORD from the west, And His glory from the rising of the sun; When the enemy comes in like a flood, The Spirit of the LORD will lift up a standard against him.*

Look at these other translations and really catch a glimpse of how powerful this standard is!

For he will come like a pent-up flood, that the breath of the LORD drives along. (NIV)

For he will come like a raging flood tide driven by the breath of the LORD. (NLT)

For he will come like a rushing stream, which the wind of the LORD drives. (ESV)

He will come like a rushing stream. The wind of the LORD pushes him. (GOD'S WORD® Translation)

As you can see from the different interpretations and translations, this is a powerful awesome force. When we lift up a standard or banner, it is not any standard, it is God's awesome standard. It is the power of Jesus Christ! In lifting a standard against the enemy it puts up a flood of the breath of God. It brings a raging, rushing, mighty and violent stream breaking all barriers down. It is like the breath and wind of God, which pushes our enemies into oblivion; they disappear at His breath!

Jesus is our standard — Romans 8:37 declares that "Yet, in all these things we are more than conquerors through him who loved us." Through Christ, we have victory over death as well as life's battles. And we don't just barely win the battles in Him — WE HAVE ALREADY WON!!! NO WEAPON FORMED AGAINST US SHALL PROSPER!

The Comma

You see, the English translation of this verse is wrong! The comma is in the wrong place. It normally reads like this: *When the Enemy comes in like a flood, the Spirit of God will raise a standard against him!* (Isaiah 59:19) But it should read like this if you read it in the original Hebrew: *When the Enemy comes in (pause, comma), like a flood the Spirit of God will raise a standard against him!* (Isaiah 59:19) See, the enemy never comes in like a flood. Remember he likes to make you think he has power over you.

Let us look at this comma or pause, and gain heavenly understanding of the position of this comma and the power when it is in its rightful place. We have to get it back where it is suppose to be. Here is my revelation on this! The comma or pause or selah is when you first surrender to God. This is when you recognize that the enemy is trying to deceive you. He is trying to get you to see that he is bigger. STOP! This is when you say "God, I surrender to your will and your life and purpose; lead me and guide me as I wait on your instruction on what I am to do now." This is following the pattern of Jesus waiting and watching to see what God wants you to do.

The comma is where the power is. It is where we get our lion's roar back. This is where our warrior spirit rises up. This is where we recognize just how awesome and powerful our God is. This is when we rise up from the depths of despair and rise from the ashes to victory. This, friend, is the power of the comma.

The power of the comma also lets all know that God the Father is never on the back foot. He never needs to make a defensive move against Satan. That is why the enemy will never come in like a flood. Only the Great I Am can create a flood of life, power and authority in your situation. The truth is when the enemy comes in, comma, *Like a Flood the Spirit of God* comes in. I'm just glad that no matter what the enemy does he is already been defeated!!!!!!! Victory was set at the cross and it's ours by faith and possession!

Like a Flood

The Scripture actually says that like a flood, the Spirit will raise up a standard against the enemy. Let me say this one more time emphatically. God the Father is never on the back foot. He never needs to make a defensive move against Satan. That is why the enemy will never come in like a flood.

First of all the enemy cannot create anything like a flood. He has no power to create. He can lie to us, cause us to see his tactics as a flood, but our enemy is defeated. Truly, we are in the midst of a war. But a war where we have already won!

God Word declares in Isaiah 43:2, *When you pass through the waters, I will be with you; And through the rivers, they shall not overflow you. When you walk through the fire, you shall not be burned, nor shall the flame burn you.*

The standard that is lifted up against the enemy of our minds, finances, families, marriages, children, employment and every area of our lives is the Word of God! Yes, God Himself. .

You and I are victors because of the victory Jesus won. You and I are conquerors because we serve the conquering King. You and I are more than conquerors! Galatians 3:27, *As many of you as have been baptized into Christ has put on Christ.* So "put on Christ." He is our supreme victory!!

1 Corinthians 15:17, *But thanks be to God! He gives us the victory through our Lord Jesus Christ.*

Be strong in the Lord and in the power of His might. Put on the whole armor of God, that you may be able to stand against the wiles of the devil. For we wrestle not against flesh and blood but against principalities, against powers, against the rulers of the darkness of this age, against spiritual hosts of wickedness in the heavenly places.

Comma and Surrender

Therefore take up the whole armor of God, that you may be able to withstand in the evil day and having done all, to stand. Let us add the comma to our warfare since our comma, our pause, is our surrender and that is power in itself. Let us add surrender as one of our weapons as we put it on each day.

I wrote a song called the power of your surrender and here are the words to it:

Your power begins with your surrender.

I offer myself up to You as a living sacrifice, wholly I surrender.

Your power begins with your surrender, let the winds of Your mercy flow.

We are seeking those things above and wholly we surrender.

Heaven, breathe on my surrender let the winds of Your mercy.

We are seeking those things above and wholly we surrender.

I Surrender, I surrender, I surrender to You!

My friend, there is true real power in surrender. Whatever you are willing to surrender is where you gain access and real power.

The Armor of God

So Stand therefore, having girded your waist with truth, having put on the breastplate of righteousness, and having shod your feet with the preparation of the gospel of peace; above all, taking the shield of faith with which you will be able to quench all the fiery darts of the wicked one.

And take the helmet of salvation, and the sword of the Spirit, which is the word of God; praying always with all prayer and supplication in the Spirit, being watchful to this end with all perseverance and supplication for all the saints. (Ephesians 6:10-18)

God's armor brings victory because it is far more than a protective covering. It is the very life of Jesus Christ Himself.

So put on the armor and when we do, Christ becomes our hiding place and our shelter in the storm, just as He was to David. Hidden in Him, you can count on His victory, for He not only covers us as a shield, He also fills our life with His life.

Remember our enemy is defeated and we are victorious. When we lift up a standard or banner, it is not any standard, it is God's awesome standard, it is the power of Jesus Christ! In lifting a standard against the enemy it puts up a flood of the breath of God. It brings a raging, rushing, mighty and violent stream breaking all barriers down. It is like the breath and wind of God, which pushes our enemies into oblivion; they disappear at His breath!

Chapter 12
DECREE WITH ABSOLUTE FAITH[1]

Worthy is the Lamb that was slain to receive power, riches
strength, wisdom, honor, glory and blessing, and grateful I am
to receive this seven-fold blessing based on the finished work of
Christ. Thus I can do what the Bible says I can do! Be what the
Bible says I can be! And have what the Bible says I can have!

I now decree, declare and affirm with absolute faith that I walk,
talk, wear, think, experience, emanate and release to others the
seven-fold blessing everywhere I go and manifest the results and
power of the New covenant of which I have been enjoined.

I replace my will with the will of God and accept the mind of
Christ and position myself to receive all things that pertain to life
and godliness through the Holy Spirit!

I am not ashamed of increase and I decree, declare and make
known to all that I'm blessed to be a blessing! To God be the
Glory!!

I decree, declare and affirm with absolute faith that God is my

---

[1] Acknowledgment to pastor R. E. Fulford for material in this chapter.

source, releasing exceedingly great power toward me everyday, in every way by Christ Jesus and the Eternal Spirit of the living God! In Jesus' name! (Ephesians 3:19)

I decree, declare and affirm with absolute faith by God's eternal Spirit of grace and mercy that I now inhabit heavenly places and sit high above all principality and power, might and dominions and every name that is named! Thus I work, walk, talk, and think in authority and exercise my right to be rich and live the abundant life style given unto me by Christ Jesus! In Jesus' name! (Ephesians 1:12-23, 2:4)

I decree, declare and affirm with absolute faith that today going forward I operate outside this worlds system and accumulate wealth, health, riches, honor and blessing supernaturally by divine providence, favor, righteousness, judgment and mercy In Jesus' name! (Philippians 4:19)

I decree, declare and affirm with absolute faith that as an heir of God and joint heir with Christ I have a right to be rich, prosperous and well satisfied in all areas of my life with plenty to give and enough to meet all needs that arise, with plenty to spare! In Jesus' name! (2 Corinthians 9:6-12)

I decree, declare and affirm with absolute faith that the divine will of God is for me to dwell in my wealthy place! Multiple channels of prosperity, riches, health, wealth, abundance, and financial increase come into, invade and saturate my life now in Jesus' name! (Deuteronomy 28:1-14)

I decree, declare and affirm with absolute faith that my hearing is acute, fine tuned, bent toward His heart and magnetized to the voice of the Holy Spirit who shall speak to me, lead and guide me into my wealthy place. Thus I will trust, follow and execute the plans of the Spirit in order to achieve my destination and inhabit this fabulous place. (Isaiah 48:15-18)

I decree, declare and affirm with absolute faith that I have arrived in my wealthy place of abundance, prosperity, riches, spiritual power, wisdom and blessing! The blessing of Abraham has exploded in my life and I now have become a channel for God's unlimited flow of supplies and a vessel prepared for His use! In Jesus' name!! (Psalm 66:12, 2 Peter 1:3-11, Galatians 3:13-14)

I decree, declare and affirm with absolute faith that God is my source using many channels, of which I am one, to bless His people and accomplish His will in the earth realm. As a channel I open myself up to receive and release by faith, healing, empowerment, salvation, wisdom, knowledge, creative ideas, increase, blessing, the anointing, discernment, love, reconciliation, restoration, deliverance, stability and grace all in Jesus' name. (Isaiah 60)

I decree, declare and affirm with absolute faith that I let the wisdom of God overshadow my spirit, mind, soul and body that I may be guided in what to say, how to say it and to whom to say it to! In Jesus' name! (Isaiah 55:11-13)

I decree, declare and affirm with absolute faith that everyday I expect, experience and manifest the miracles of the Kingdom, which validate, vindicate and confirm the Word of God in the earth realm! (Psalm 62:5)

I decree, declare and affirm with absolute faith that I walk, operate, pray and speak through the Spirit. I see, hear and manifest the things of the Spirit through the fruit and gifts of the Spirit of God and through my spiritual connection with the Kingdom of God I receive and I am entitled to and embrace the prepared blessings that have been reserved, revealed, transferred and released into my life, family and church! (1 Corinthians 2:9-12)

I decree, declare and affirm with absolute faith that today forward I believe all things are possible through the anointing, the Word and recognizing God as my source. (Luke 1:37)

I decree, declare and affirm with absolute faith that today my heart is filled with the presence of God and will forever provide a place for His habitation, demonstration and power! (2 Corinthians 4:7, 6:16)

I decree, declare and affirm with absolute faith that I walk under the anointing of Christ, which has destroyed all yokes, links, chains and strongholds connected to my life and all those I connect with. Setting all totally, completely and absolutely free financially, physically, spiritually and emotionally!! (Isaiah 10:27, Jonah 8:32,36, 2 Corinthians 10:3-6)

I decree, declare and affirm with absolute faith that today I flow in the anointing of Christ, grace of God and empowerment of the Holy Spirit for the fulfillment of His will for my life and advancement of humanity family and the Kingdom. (Isaiah 11:1-4, Luke 10:19-20, Acts 1:8)

I decree, declare and affirm with absolute faith that the spirit of fear, doubt, unbelief, disobedience and deception are broken and eliminated from my life, family, ministry and church. Thus I now flow with the Trinity in peace, power, wisdom, understanding, knowledge, gifts, skills, talents of the Kingdom of God for the manifestation of His Glory in the earth realm! (John 7:38-39, 16:13-16)

I decree, declare and affirm with absolute faith that from this day forward Ill never be broke again – not another day of my life, for the anointing has destroyed all yokes, chains, hinders, restrictions, obstacles and dams that have blocked all forms of increase, prosperity, advancement, elevations and promotions that were ordained for the fulfillment of God's will in my life, family and church! (Isaiah 10:27, 2 Corinthians 8:9).

I decree, declare and affirm with absolute faith that the Lord is my shepherd and I shall not want! He restores my soul, anoints my head, mind and spirit and makes my soul overflow with joy, peace, power, the anointing, love, vision, dreams, directions, favor and patience. (Psalm 23)

I decree, declare and affirm with absolute faith that I, through the anointing of God, shall not want, have, lack, experience poverty or suffer need but shall be completely supplied with all blessings both natural and spiritual to fulfill my destiny! Thus I attract abundance in all forms, experience financial freedom, become a lender, the head above only, and obtain all resources from God my only source, in the form of gifts, donations, rewards, grants, business transactions, miracles, divine manifestations, wealth transfers and the like that I may excel, advance the Kingdom of God and establish His covenant in the earth realm and bring Glory to His name! (1 Chronicles 29:11-12, Deuteronomy 28:1-14)

I decree, declare and affirm with absolute faith that today supernatural debt cancellation has taken place in my life, ministry, family and church. Wealth, riches, prosperity, all currencies and financial elevation comes into my life now without delay in Jesus' name!! (Genesis 12:1-3, 13:1-2)

Chapter 13

DECREES TO KNOW AND MANIFEST

Father, I hear Your voice, know Your heart, see Your beauty and experience Your lovingkindness in the morning. Father, I trust in Your heart and Your passion over me. Cause me to know the way in which I should walk, for I lift up my soul to You.

Teach me to do Your will, for You are my God; Your Spirit is good.

Synchronize my life with Your perfect will, agenda and calendar.

Superimpose Your will over the will of evil spirits and evil men.

Empower me to serve You in holiness and righteousness.

Grant me divine Kingdom asylum and diplomatic immunity from evil that seeks to imprison and entrap me.

Since my time is in Your hands, You will deliver me from the hands of my enemies and from those who persecute me.

Dismantle evil powers working to frustrate my day, assignments, and activities.

Frustrate the arrows shot toward me by day and cause the terror by night to cease. Rescue me from my enemies, for I hide myself in You. Cause the east winds of judgment to blow into the enemy's camp. Stop the diabolical cyclones and demonic winds designed to bring shipwreck and disaster into my life.

Cause divine and fresh winds of the Holy Spirit to blow. Let the west winds of replenishment, the north winds of abundance, and the south winds of restoration and supernatural supply blow profusely.

Assign angels as my divine escorts and supernatural security. Let them marshal the boundaries and borders of my spheres of influence. Let them dismantle and destroy satanic strongholds and dispossess satanic squatters.

Close the gates of death and seal up the doors of affliction and torment.

Open divine gates of access to new doors of opportunity; windows of divine inspiration, insight, and revelation; paths of righteousness; avenues of success and prosperity; and channels for transition and deliverance.

Teach me Your way, so that I may know how to conduct my affairs in the most discerning, expeditious, and fiscally wise manner.

Open my eyes to cutting edge technologies, methodologies, tactics, and strategies that can aid me in doing Your will.

Father, allow only those with divine assignments to be drawn to me.

Let Holy Spirit and His wisdom, understanding, counsel, might, knowledge, the fear of the Lord, and prophetic insight be upon me today.

Grant me the ability to hear clearly as You give me insight, witty ideas, and creative inventions.

Open my ears and let Your Word inspire me to righteousness.

Open my ears to the symphonic movements of the Spirit with clear, crisp transmission.

Cause my spiritual eyes to function with 20/20 vision for the correct insight, understanding, and interpretations of the choreographic movements of Your heart.

Let not my eyes be seduced by the spirit of covetousness or my mind by the pride of life.

Holy Spirit, give me new ways of living and better strategies; upgrade me with Kingdom technology and Kingdom methodology; I receive the supernatural discipline to implement them today.

Father, place the anointing of a warrior upon me. Every domain and system that You have assigned me, I confiscate from the enemy. I release the law of dispossession; every satanic or demonic squatter that is on my land, property, or territory, I command to go in the name of Jesus. I am more than a conqueror!

Strengthen the hedge of protection around my life, my possessions, my family, my friends and associates, and my ministry.

I remind principalities, powers, and familiar spirits that they have no right to touch my life in any way, for I am in covenant with God and hidden in the secret place of the Most High.

Holy Spirit, lead and guide me into all truth. Order my steps according to Your Word and Your original plan and purpose for my life.

I release my name into the atmosphere & decree and declare:

I have a good reputation. There are no negative stigmas attached to me.

I am a campaigner of empowerment. My name is associated with:

Greatness - Integrity - Nobility - Righteousness - Holiness - Morality - Ethical dealings - Honesty - Humility - Grace - Love - Joy - Peace - Longsuffering - Gentleness - Meekness - Faith - Goodness - Self-control - Generosity - Fairness - Vision - Wisdom - Wealth - Luxury - Extravagance - Health - Intelligence - Prosperity - Knowledge - Prayer and Spiritual Power - The anointing - Kingdom wisdom - Kingdom undertakings and Success

I release my name and all that is assigned to me and associated with me into the atmosphere.

Allow prayer warriors to pick me up in the realm of the spirit and pray, reinforcing my hedge of protection. Let them stand in the prophetic and intercessory gap for all that is assigned to me and associated with me.

Chapter 14
IN JESUS' NAME I AM

I am a Son of God.

I am saved by grace.

I am born of incorruptible seed.

The Blood redeems me.

I am forgiven of all my sins.

I am a new creature in Christ.

I am redeemed from the curse of the law.

I am beloved of God.

I am seated in heavenly places in Christ Jesus.

I am a part of the royal priesthood.

I am a member of a chosen generation.

I am an ambassador for Christ, the light of the world.

I am a citizen of the Kingdom of Heaven.

I am a joint heir with Jesus.

I am accepted in the Beloved.

I am complete in Him.

I am crucified with Christ.

I am alive with Christ.

I am free from condemnation.

I am reconciled to God.

I am justified by faith.

I am qualified to share in Jesus' inheritance.

I am a fellow citizen with the saints and the household of God.

I am a significant, contributing member of the body of Christ.

I am the temple of the Holy Spirit.

I am the salt of the earth.

I am the bride of Christ.

I am sealed with the Holy Spirit of promise.

I am a saint.

I am the elect of God.

I am established by grace.

I am drawn near to God by the Blood of Christ.

I am victorious through Christ.

I am purposely built and uniquely designed for success.

I am set free.

I am a disciple of Christ.

I am a steward of great wealth.

I am a visionary.

I am the head and not the tail.

I am above and not beneath.

I am first and not last.

I am strong in the Lord.

I am more than a conqueror.

I am firmly rooted, built up, and established in the faith.

I am abounding in a spirit of thanksgiving.

I am spiritually circumcised.

I am the righteousness of God.

I am a partaker of His divine nature.

I am an heir according to the promise.

I am called of God.

I am fearfully and wonderfully made.

I am the apple of my Father's eye.

I am healed by the stripes of Jesus Christ.

I am being changed into His image.

I am fathered from above.

I am filled with the Holy Spirit.

I am God's workmanship created in Christ Jesus.

I am delivered from the power of darkness.

I am translated into the Kingdom of God.

I am hidden in the secret place of the Most High.

I am defensively clad with the armor of God.

I am offensively equipped with the sword of the Spirit, which is the Word of God.

I am protected by heavenly angels.

I am an overcomer.

I am transformed by the renewing of my mind.

I am God's representative in the earth realm.

I am unable to be touched by evil.

I am empowered to successfully engage in spiritual warfare and achieve victory.

I am forgiven of all my sins and redeemed through the Blood.

I am blessed with all spiritual blessings in heavenly places.

I am chosen of God, holy and blameless before Him in love.

I am complete in Christ.

I am overtaken with His blessings.

Chapter 15
HEART DECREES OF PASSION & FIRE

My heart grows hot within me, and as I meditate, the fire burns; then I speak with my tongue.

My tongue is the pen of a skillful writer. I write the words upon the tablet of my heart.

My heart is stirred by a noble theme as I recite my verses for the King.

The Holy Spirit is my teacher and guide. He reveals the Word to me so that I can understand it.

I have been enriched in all my knowledge and in all my speech.

I do not put out the Spirit's fire. In fact, I fan into flame the gift of God, which is in me.

I have the spirit of revelation and knowledge. I am coming to know Christ better everyday.

I have the glorious inheritance working inside of me.

I have the same power of God that was used to raise Christ from the dead. I have resurrection power within me.

I cast my cares upon the Lord, because He cares for me and watches over me affectionately. He has my best interest at heart.

I hunger for righteousness. I am filled with all the spiritual blessings in heavenly places.

I meditate in the Word day and night, so that I can recognize God's will and then act upon it. As I practice the Word, I am blessed in everything I do.

I esteem my words and treat them with respect. More than that, I esteem God and His Word above everything.

My words are increasing in power and force, because I let nothing come out of my mouth except what is helpful in building up others according to their needs.

I love my words. I reap my words. My words are working to produce life.

The Spirit is turning up the power of my words, because I speak God's words.

God's Word is the final authority in my life. I do not accept anything that does not live up with God's Word.

I reject all tradition that does not conform to God's Word.

I refuse to say anything that would disrespect God's authority.

I have a merry heart, and it does well like medicine.

I am more than a conqueror through Christ who loves me.

I have faith in my words. I believe what I say comes to pass.

The Word is near me. It is in my mouth and in my heart. It is the word of faith that I proclaim.

I have been created in God's image. I am a spirit, I have a soul, and I live in a body.

God has given me dominion. I have the power and right to govern and control.

My words are spirit, and they are life.

My first job is to cooperate with God in naming the kind of life I will have.

God's Word is not void of power. It has the ability within itself to reproduce. I make God's Word my words.

I have been made complete in Him. I am growing up in my salvation. My faith is growing exceedingly.

God is faithful. What He said, He is able to bring to pass.

God's Word comes out of my mouth, and it accomplishes what God desires and achieves the purpose for which He sent it.

I desire to please my heavenly Father by imitating Him.

I will walk in love and walk by faith in God's Word.

I do not go beyond God's Word. I speak not worldly words, but I speak godly words.

Whatever is of a good report, I speak it and think it.

My God shall supply all of my needs according to His riches in glory in Christ Jesus.

He is my shepherd, so I don't have a care in the world.

I can say what God has said. Because He has said, "Never will I leave you and never will I forsake you," I can say with boldness, "The Lord is my helper; I will not be afraid. What can man do to me?"

All things are possible with God, and I choose to believe in Him.

The world may trust in horses and chariots, but I trust in the name of the Lord.

His name is a strong tower; I run to it and am safe.

Like Mary, I receive God's Word inside my heart, I meditate on it, and it becomes flesh.

I will not speak what comes to my mind but will speak what is in God's mind.

God's Word will not return to Him void, but will accomplish what He desires and achieve the purpose for which He sent it.

I plant the imperishable Word of God into my life and into others. It never fails to produce.

I can trust in God's Word because it is impossible for God to lie. Let every man be a liar, and let God be true.

I prophesy according to the measure of faith within me. I take God's Word and speak it out of my mouth before it happens.

My faith comes by hearing as I listen to the Word of God.

The hand of the Lord is upon me. As I prophesy, great things are happening.

I am a vessel for the Lord. He uses me as He sees fit. He is the potter, and I am the clay.

Though the outward man is decaying, my inward man is being renewed day by day. My youth is renewed like the eagles. Like Moses, my eyes are not growing dim nor is my strength gone.

I do not forget any of the Lord's benefits. He forgives all my iniquities, and He heals all my diseases. He satisfies my desires with good things. He redeems my life from the pit and crowns me with love and compassion.

I release Christ in me, the hope of glory.

I hear the sound of an abundance of blessings. It is coming my way! Glory be to God!

I live by faith, not by sight. It doesn't matter what I feel like; I am a king.

I am a king. I reign in life through Jesus Christ.

I am in charge of my life through God's power. I am not subject to the world's troubles.

God Works Through My Words

I am a priest and a king.

I reign in life through Jesus Christ.

I rule over Satan and his house. I tread on serpents and scorpions. Nothing they try to do can harm me. I am under God's protection. I declare Psalm 91.

I have the keys of the Kingdom of God. What I bind, Heaven binds. What I loose, heave looses.

I bind all forces of evil in my life. I loose all the blessings of God into my life.

I put a guard over my mouth. I refuse to say anything wrong. I speak only God's Word.

My body lines up to the words of my mouth. What I say is what I get. My body works perfectly, just the way God intended it to work.

I don't verbalize my fears. I verbalize only my faith.

It doesn't matter what trials come my way; I only speak what is a good report.

The report of the Lord is I'm healed, I'm blessed, and I have victory through faith in Jesus Christ.

I am raised up with Christ and made to sit with Him in heavenly places. I am on top of the world.

I have no reason to fear the future. God has plans to prosper me and not harm me. He has plans to give me hope and a future.

I am following God's plan for my life.

I know where I'm going because I have God's wisdom in my life. Jesus has given me wisdom from God.

I am filled with good things by the fruit of my lips.

Life and blessings are on my tongue. I speak only the good and not the bad.

The life I am now living is the result of the words I spoke in the past. So, today I am speaking good things; later my life will become these good words, which I am speaking today!

I will not walk in the negative words that people have spoken over my life. I bind those negative words from my life.

I can do all things through Christ who strengthens me.

I will live and not die, and I will declare the glory of the Lord.

I am a world overcomer.

Greater is the Holy Spirit who is in me than the devil who is in the world.

All things work together for my good because I love God and am called according to His good purpose.

Jesus bore the thorns to redeem me from the curse. I can produce good fruit.

I am a fruit-bearing branch of the vine of Jesus Christ.

In Him I live, move, and have my being. I am a new creature in Christ Jesus.

I am not going to let things happen to me. I am going to cause good things to happen by co-creating with God, by releasing His heart by my voice to bring life to my today and my future.

My success has nothing to do with luck or chance; it has to do with Jesus. He is my Lord! He is my boss.

I am a new creature in Christ Jesus. The old me has died. The new me is full of joy, peace, and love.

Angels protect me and encamp around me because I trust in the Lord.

God is good and never brings tragedy into my life.

I am blessed with all spiritual blessings in heavenly places in Christ Jesus.

God has predestined me to be conformed into the image of His dear Son.

I am adopted into God's family. I can call God "Father."

I am one of His chosen ones. He picked me for His family because He wanted to.

God has set before me life and death. So, I choose life.

There is now no condemnation for me because I am in Christ Jesus. I have chosen Christ because He has chosen me!

Healing

I believe in divine healing.

I receive healing according to my faith.

Jesus heals all my diseases and sicknesses. He is still the same yesterday, today, and forever.

I make Jesus my doctor and best physician.

Surely, Jesus took up my infirmities and carried my sorrow. By His stripes I am healed.

God is not the author of sickness and disease. Satan is the oppressor, and I resist Satan now.

I forbid Satan to put any disease in my body. My body is the temple of the Holy Spirit.

I resist all symptoms. I live by faith, not by sight.

I am in this world, but I am not of this world. I am delivered from this present evil world.

A merry heart does well to me like medicine.

The joy of the Lord is my strength. The glory of the Lord is my rear guard.

God's Word is life and health unto all my flesh.

Every part of my body functions perfectly. My eyes work well. My ears work well. My muscles work well. My heart works well. My bones work well. All my organs, tissues, cells, ligaments, and hormones and blood work well.

The Spirit that raised Christ from the dead is dwelling inside me and is making alive my mortal body.

Jesus paid for my healing, so I'm walking in health.

Blessings, Wealth and Riches

I know the grace of my Lord Jesus Christ. Though He was rich, yet for my sake He became poor so that I could become rich.

I am rich. I am abundantly supplied. I am highly effective. I am a success in every way.

I use the power of God to meet any need. I do not lack any good thing.

I am a seed of Abraham, so I am blessed along with him. I have his blessings. I walk in the blessings of Abraham.

I remember the Lord, for it is He who gives me the ability to create wealth.

I am blessed so that I can be a blessing.

I refuse to allow the spirit of greed to control my life.

I am a tither and give. I give, and it is given back to me in good measure, pressed down, shaken together, and running over.

The Lord opens up the windows of Heaven and pours out on me so many blessings that I have to yell, "That's enough!"

The devil is rebuked from touching my finances.

Christ has redeemed me from the curse of poverty, so I refuse to be poor.

Poverty is underneath my feet.

I am the head and not the tail. I lend unto many, but I do not have to borrow.

Jesus is the Guarantee of all the promises of God. He makes sure that I enjoy all my privileges and rights under the new agreement.

I live under a better covenant, a covenant that has been ratified by the Blood of Jesus.

Faith, Favor, Grace and Righteousness

I am the righteousness of God in Christ Jesus.

I am growing in the grace of God. I am experiencing God's unmerited favor. I have favor with God and with men.

People look upon me with kindness because I see people as my friends, not as enemies.

I approach the throne of grace with boldness. I have a right to the Presence of God.

I receive grace every time I ask for it. I ask, and I receive.

I am as bold as a lion. I refuse to fear anything. I do not fear even when I hear bad news. My heart is fixed on trusting in the Lord.

My faith may be tested, but I will pass the test.

I inherit all the promises of God through faith and patience.

I will not become bitter toward anyone, even if they slander me. I will pray for those who persecute me.

I'm not afraid of the devil or his schemes. I have dominion over him by the power of the Blood of Jesus.

I fear not because God has not given me a spirit of fear, but of love, power, and a sound mind.

Many are the afflictions of the righteous, but the Lord delivers me from them all.

In this world I shall have tribulations, but I am of good cheer, because Christ has overcome the world.

I am a world overcomer because I live by faith, not by sight.

I have mountain-moving faith. I speak to mountains, and they obey me.

I have Godlike faith. I believe; therefore, I speak. I have the spirit of faith. This faith overcomes obstacles.

I put on God's fighting clothes. I put on the belt of truth. I have my feet covered with the preparation of the gospel of peace.
I have my breastplate of righteousness in place. I put on the helmet of salvation and take up the sword of the spirit, which is the Word of God. And above all else, I use the shield of faith to guard me from the arrows of the evil one.

I am shielded by God's faith and power.

I am a participant in the divine nature. I have God's faith, God's peace, God's joy, God's love, God's patience, and God's strength.

I am regenerated. I have God's spiritual genes. If you've seen me, you've seen the Father. As Christ is, so am I in this world.

I am growing up in my salvation. I have the joy of my salvation.

My faith is growing exceedingly fast.

I am learning to listen to God's voice and obey His Word.

I refuse to say anything that I don't hear my Father saying. I speak only what I hear my Father speak.

God has a wonderful plan for me. He plans to prosper me and not to harm me.

He plans to give me hope and a future.

I trust God. I do not fear the future, because God is in control of my life.

Chapter 16

ACCORDING TO
YOUR WORD

Let me show you how to personalize Scripture and how to apply it to your everyday life. You will find that the Word will explode with faith and life as you speak it and make it personal. Below I show you how you can change Scripture by changing verb tenses and pronouns. Let's look at this passage of Scripture as an example.

He sent from on high, He took me;
He drew me out of many waters,
He delivered me from my strong enemy
And from those who hated me, for they were too mighty for me.
They confronted me in the day of my calamity,
But the Lord was my stay;
He brought me forth also into a broad place;
He rescued me, because He delighted in me.
(Psalm 18:16-19, NASB)

Prayer #1

Thank You, Lord, that You have sent from on high. You have taken me and drawn me out of many waters. Lord, You have delivered me from my strong enemy and from those who hate me, for they were too mighty for me. They confronted me in the day of my calamity, but Lord, You were my stay. You brought me forth into a broad place. You have rescued me because You delight in me.

Prayer #2

Thank You, Lord, for Your saving arm that reached from Heaven and drew me from the flood waters of fear that attempted to sweep me away when I heard the doctors' grim report. You have delivered me from the fear of _____ and from the fact of whatever disease _____, both enemies that were too strong for me, if left to my own strength.

You have delivered me from the thief that came to steal away my life prematurely. Lord, You have delivered me from the enemy of my soul who despises me because I live and have my being in You.

The spirit of death leered at me, confronted me with destruction in the day of my calamity that day in the doctor's office, but You, Lord, prevailed.

You are my support. Because You delight in me, You not only delivered me, but have brought me out into a broad place of rich fulfillment. Alleluia!

Prayer #3

Lord, You heard from Heaven and have rescued me. You have drawn me out of the waters of fear and chaos that threatened my sanity in time of challenge. You have delivered me from my strong enemy of _____ or the enemy of my body named _____. And, You have delivered me from the enemy of my soul, named satan. They both confronted me in the day of my calamity. They confronted me with the threats yet they were too strong for me. But You, Lord, were my support. Nothing is too strong for You! You have delivered me because You delight in me. And, You have brought me out into a broad place of fulfillment and satisfaction.

Meditate on Scripture. Spend time with it. Then you will find yourself making this kind of personal application for yourself.

For instance, "My enemy is financial lack which is threatening me with bankruptcy."

Can you feel the life and power of these verses as you pray them? Prayer affirmations of faith like this:

- Strengthen and expand your faith

- Renew your mind according to the truths of God and nourish and strengthen your spirit

Chapter 17
DECREE PSALM 91

[1] I dwell in the secret place of the Most High. I abide under the shadow of the Almighty.

[2] I will say of the LORD, "He is my refuge and my fortress; My God, in Him I will trust."

[3] Surely He shall deliver me from the snare of the fowler and from the perilous pestilence.

[4] He shall cover me with His feathers, and under His wings I shall take trust; His truth shall be my shield and buckler.

[5] I shall not be afraid of the terror by night, or of the arrow that flies by day,

[6] Nor of the pestilence that walks in darkness, Nor of the destruction that lays waste at noonday.

[7] A thousand may fall at my side, and ten thousand at my right hand but it shall not come nigh me.

⁸ Only with your eyes shall I behold, and see the reward of the wicked.

⁹ Because I have made the LORD, which is my refuge, even the Most High, my habitation,

¹⁰ There shall No evil shall befall me, neither shall any plague come near my dwelling;

¹¹ For He shall give His angels charge over me, to keep me in all your ways.

¹² They shall bear me up in their hands, lest I dash my foot against a stone.

¹³ You shall tread upon the lion and the adder, the young lion and the dragon shall I trample underfoot.

¹⁴ Because I have set my love upon You, therefore He will deliver me; He will set me on high, because I have known His name.

¹⁵ I shall call upon Him, and He will answer me; He will be with me in trouble; He will deliver me and honor me.

¹⁶ With long life He will satisfy me, and show me His Y'shua (salvation).

Chapter 18
DECREE EPHESIANS 1

Grace and peace are given to me from God, my Father and my Lord Jesus Christ. He has blessed me with every spiritual blessing in the heavenly places. He chose me in Him before the foundation of the world, that I should be holy and without blame before Him in love. He predestined me into adoption through Jesus Christ to Himself, according to the good pleasure of His Will. He made me accepted in the Beloved.

In Him, I have redemption through His Blood and the forgiveness of sins according to the richness of His Grace, which He has made abound towards me in all wisdom and prudence. He makes known to me the mystery of His Will, according to His good pleasure, which He purposed in Himself. In the dispensation of the fullness of time, He will gather together in one all things in Christ, both which are in Heaven and on earth in Him.

In Him, I have obtained an inheritance. I have been predestined according to the counsel of His Will. In Him, I have trusted and heard the Word of Truth, the gospel of my salvation. I have believed and I am sealed with the Holy Spirit of Promise, who has guaranteed my inheritance until the redemption of the purchased possession to the praise of His Glory.

I do not cease to give thanks for my faith. I make mention of myself in my prayers so that the God of my Lord Jesus Christ, my Father of Glory, may give me the spirit of wisdom and revelation through the knowledge of Jesus Christ. I pray for the eyes of my understanding to be unveiled so that I may know the hope of His calling in my life and the riches of the Glory of His inheritance to me. His exceedingly great power is working in me because I believe. This same power is what raised Jesus from the dead and seated Him at the Right Hand of the Father in heavenly places.

He is far above every principality, power, might and dominion, as well as every name that is named not only in this age, but even in the ages to come. He has put all things under His feet and gave Him to be the head over all things to the church, which is His Body, the fullness of Him who fills all in all

Chapter 19

DECREES OF POWER & SCRIPTURE

"Let integrity and uprightness preserve me; for I wait on You" (Psalm 25:21). *"Make me to know my end, and what is the measure of my days, that I may know how frail I am."* (Psalm 39:4)

Father, in the name of Jesus, I decree and declare:

That my spirit man is clad with the armor of the Lord and the armor of light. That Your Kingdom is my priority and Your assignment is my pleasure. Let Your Kingdom come and Your will be done on the earth as it is in Heaven.

I function and conduct my life's affairs according to Your original plan and purpose for me.

I walk in Your timing. You are the one and true God, who makes everything work together and who works all things for good through Your most excellent harmonies.

Cause my will to work in perfect harmony with Yours.

Evil shall not come near my dwelling, since I dwell in the secret place of the Most High God and dwell under the shadow of the Almighty.

I cause demonic destiny altering activities to cease. I take hold of the ends of the earth and shake evil out of its place.

I break evil and inappropriate thought patterns in my mind.

I speak peace into my life, relationships, ministry, workplace, and business.

Everything that is misaligned I command to come into divine alignment.

I have the mind of Christ and therefore seek things above and not beneath.

I ascend into new realms of power and authority and access new dimensions of divine revelation.

I will not backslide or look back into old ways, old methodologies, or old strategies unless directed by You to do so.

I wear the helmet of salvation to protect my mind from negative thoughts that would derail Your purposes and plans for me.

Truth protects my integrity, righteousness protects my reputation, the gospel of peace guides my every step, the shield of faith secures my future and destiny, and the sword of the Spirit grants me dominion and authority.

I decree and declare a prophetic upgrading of my thought life. I cancel the effect of negative, self-defeating thought processes and patterns and put them under my feet.

I possess a Kingdom paradigm which grants me new ways of thinking, new ways of working, and new ways of living. New cycles of victory, success, and prosperity will replace old cycles of failure, poverty, and death in my life.

I now have a new, refreshed, cutting edge Kingdom mentality.

At Your Word, as a Kingdom trailblazer, I pioneer new territory.

Everything that pertains to my life and godliness and everything prepared for me before the foundation of the world must be released in its correct time and season. I command everything to be released in Jesus' name.

I declare that there will be no substitutes, no holdups, no setbacks, and no delays.

Since Your Word is a lamp unto my feet and a light unto my path, I shall neither stumble nor fall.

Today I am blessed; there is no lack. All my needs are met. I am out of debt, and I have more than enough to give over and above all my needs.

I am excited; my spirit is ignited; I walk in favor
with God and man.

I am a success oriented individual, and everything I touch turns
to "prophetic gold."

I am a successful business owner; an entrepreneur who provides
good jobs to others.

All financial doors are opened, and all financial channels are
free. Endless bounty comes to me.

Sufficient is Your provision for today.

I am healed and Spirit filled; sickness and disease are
far from me.

I have buying power on my dollar and I live in prosperity.

I confess that I only progress; I experience no setbacks and live a
life filled with success

I will persist until I succeed.

I walk in dominion and authority.

My life is characterized by liberty.

There is no slackness in my hand. Where I stand, God gives me the land.

The blessings of the Lord make me rich and I am daily loaded with benefits.

I am living my most blessed and best days now.

I am crowned with God's love and mercy.

With all good things He satisfies me.

My home is a haven of peace and heavenly encounter.

I do my work as unto the Lord with diligence and in the spirit of excellence.

My home, business, departments, and ministries function smoothly and efficiently.

The Lord gives me wisdom, knowledge, and understanding as to how to do my work more effectively, professionally, and accurately.

The Lord gives me all the right people to work with and for me. Together we work as unto the Lord.

Relationships will come to me that are assigned to enhance my life and ministry for this season.

I call forth every individual and resource assigned to assist me in the fulfillment of my Kingdom assignment during this season.

I attract only the things, thoughts, people, and resources suitable to undergird and facilitate God's original plan and purpose for my life.

All who know me, meet me, work with me, and have any kind of formal or informal relationship with me favors me.

I work according to Your daily agenda and perform for an audience of one the Lord Jesus Christ.

My Work Is My Worship

You are teaching me how to improve my productivity to work smarter and more efficiently.

I always function with an outstanding attitude and produce superior work.

I maximize my potential and move boldly toward my destiny.

You empower me to make positive and significant deposits in other people's lives.

I seek divine opportunities and occasions to help others succeed.

I am a purpose driven, Kingdom principled, success oriented individual, and I refuse to be distracted by insignificant things and people.

Let favor, well wishes, ambassadorial courtesies, kindness, and support be extended to me by all who are assigned to me meet me, know me, and interact with me.

I do not procrastinate. I act now, without hesitation, anxiety, or fear.

I excel in all things, at all times, with all people, under every circumstance.

I will judge nothing and no one prematurely. I celebrate Your creativity in the diversity of ethnicities, nationalities, and humanity.

I am adaptable and flexible and make needed adjustments. I am in the perfect place for You to bless me.

I am Fruitful in Every Good Work

I have power to gain wealth.

Wherever I go, systems, institutions, cultures, environments, legislation, codes, ordinances, regulations, and policies adjust to accommodate my divine purpose.

My relationships are fruitful and mutually beneficial.

I am celebrated and loved by all who come in contact with me.

Everything about me is changing for the best.

I am gaining new territories; new emotional territory, new intellectual territory, new business territory, new spiritual territory, new ministerial territory, and new financial territory.

I am healthy and physically fit.

Sickness and disease are far from me.

My mind is fortified and resolute.

My emotions are sound and stable.

My faith is steadfast and unfaltering

The zeal of the Lord fills my soul and spirit.

Let there be no demonic encroachment. Let there be no satanic squatters in the name of Jesus. Get off my property, get off my territory, get out of my sphere of influence, get out of my family, get out of my relationships, get out of my finances, get out of my body and get out of my mind.

I command mountains to be removed and to be cast into the sea.

Father, I wait to see Your finished product. I look forward to the day that I will be transformed into the image of Your dear Son. My heart's deepest desire is to be like Him.

I seal these declarations in the name of Jesus, my Lord and Savior. Now unto Him that is able to do exceedingly abundantly above all that I could ask or imagine, according to the power that works in me; to Him who is able to keep me from falling, and to present me faultless before the presence of His glory with exceeding joy, and to sustain my body, soul, and spirit; to the almighty God my heavenly Father, the King eternal, immortal, invisible, the only wise God be honor and glory forever and ever.

[Spend a few moments in praise and thanksgiving knowing that God has heard and will respond.]

Hallelujah! I praise You, God. Amen!

Chapter 20
I AM IN CHRIST

Since I am in Christ, by the grace of God I have been justified-completely forgiven and made righteous. (Romans 5:1)

I died with Christ and died to the power of sin's rule over my life. (Romans 6:1-6)

I am free forever from condemnation. (Romans 8:1)

I have been placed into Christ by God's doing. (1 Corinthians 1:30)

I have received the Spirit of God into my life that I might know the things freely given to me by God. (1 Corinthians 2:12)

I have been given the mind of Christ (1 Corinthians 2:16). I have been bought with a price; I am not my own; I belong to God. (1 Corinthians 6:19-20)

I have been made righteous. (2 Corinthians 5:21)

I have been established, anointed and sealed by God in Christ, and I have been given the Holy Spirit as a pledge guaranteeing my inheritance to come. (2 Corinthians 1:21; Ephesians 1:13-14)

Since I have died, I no longer live for myself, but for Christ. (2 Corinthians 5:14-15)

I have been crucified with Christ and it is no longer I who live, but Christ who lives in me. The life I am now living is Christ's life. (Galatians 2:20)

I have been blessed with every spiritual blessings. (Ephesians 1:3)

I was chosen in Christ before the foundation of the world to be holy and am without blame before Him. (Ephesians 1:4)

I was predestined to be adopted as God's son. (Ephesians 1:5)

I have been redeemed and forgiven, and I am a recipient of His lavish grace.

I have been made alive together with Christ. (Ephesians 2:5)

I have been raised up and seated with Christ in Heaven. (Ephesians 2:6)

I have direct access to God through the Spirit.
(Ephesians 2:18)

I may approach God with boldness, freedom and confidence.
(Ephesians 3:12)

I have been rescued from the domain of Satan's rule and
transferred to the Kingdom of Christ. (Colossians 1:13)

I have been redeemed and forgiven of all my sins. The debt
against me has been cancelled (Colossians 1:14). Christ Himself
is in me. (Colossians 1:27)

I am firmly rooted in Christ and am now being built in Him.
(Colossians 2:7)

I have been buried, raised and made alive with Christ.
(Colossians 2:12-13)

I died with Christ and I have been raised up with Christ. My
life is now hidden with Christ in God. Christ is now my life.
(Colossians 3:1-4)

I have been given a spirit of power, love and self-discipline. (2
Timothy 1:7)

I have been made complete in Christ. (Colossians 2:10)

I have been saved and set apart according to God's doing. (2 Timothy 1:9; Titus 3:5)

I have been spiritually circumcised. My old unregenerate nature has been removed. (Colossians 2:11)

I have the right to come boldly before the throne of God to find mercy and grace in the time of need. (Hebrews 4:16)

Chapter 21
I DECREE HE IS

In Genesis, Jesus is the Ram at Abraham's altar.

In Exodus, He is the Passover Lamb.

In Leviticus, He is the High Priest.

In Numbers, He is the Cloud by day and Pillar of Fire by night.

In Deuteronomy, He is the City of our Refuge.

In Joshua, He is the Scarlet Thread out of Rahab's window.

In Judges, He is our Judge.

In Ruth, He is our Kinsman Redeemer.

In 1 and 2 Samuel, He is our Trusted Prophet.

In Kings and Chronicles, He is our Reigning King.

In Ezra, He is our Faithful Scribe.

In Nehemiah, He is the Rebuilder of everything that is broken.

In Esther, He is the Mordecai sitting faithful at the gate.

In Job He is our Redeemer that ever lives.

In Psalms, He is my Shepherd, I shall not want.

In Proverbs and Ecclesiastes, He is our Wisdom.

In the Song of Solomon He is the Beautiful Bridegroom.

In Isaiah He is the Suffering Prophet.

In Jeremiah and Lamentations, He is the Weeping Prophet.

In Ezekiel He is the wonderful Four-Faced Man.

In Daniel He is the Fourth man in the midst of the fiery furnace.

In Hosea, He is my Love that is forever faithful.

In Joel, He is the Baptizer of the Holy Spirit.

In Amos, He is our Burden Bearer.

In Obadiah, He is our Savior.

In Jonah, He is the great foreign Missionary that takes the word of God into all the world.

In Micah, He is the Messenger with beautiful feet.

In Nahum, He is the Avenger.

In Habakkuk, He is the Watchman that is ever praying for revival.

In Zephaniah, He is the Lord Mighty to serve.

In Haggai, He is the Restorer of our lost heritage.

In Zechariah, He is our fountain.

In Malachi, He is the Son of righteousness with healing in His wings.

In Matthew, He is the Christ, the Son of the Living God.

In Mark, He is the Miracle worker.

In Luke, He is the Son of Man.

In John, He is the Door by which everyone of us must enter.

In Acts, He is the shining Light that appears to Saul on the road to Damascus.

In Romans, He is our Justifier.

In 1 Corinthians, He is our Resurrection.

In 2 Corinthians, He is our sin Bearer.

In Galatians, He Redeems us from the Law.

In Ephesians, He is our unsearchable Riches.

In Philippians, He supplies our every need.

In Colossians, He is the Fullness of the Godhead bodily.

In 1 and 2 Thessalonians, He is our soon Coming King.

In 1 and 2 Timothy He is the Mediator between God and man.

In Titus, He is our Blessed Hope.

In Philemon, He is a Friend that sticks closer than a brother.

In Hebrews, He is the Blood of the Everlasting Covenant.

In James, He is the Lord that heals the sick.

In 1 and 2 Peter, He is our Chief Shepherd.

In 1,2 and 3 John, it is Jesus Who has the tenderness of Love.

In Jude, He is the Lord coming with 10,000 saints.

In Revelation, He is the King of Kings and Lord of Lords

Chapter 22

HALLOWING THE NAMES OF GOD

Psalm 30:22, *We are waiting for Yahweh; He is our help and our shield, For in Him our heart rejoices. In His holy name we trust. Yahweh, let your faithful love rest on us. As our hope has rested in You.*

I thank You God that You are the Alpha, the Omega, the beginning and the end. You are the first and the last, the Creator of all things and that You have created today for me.

Psalms 103, *Bless the Lord, O my soul: and all that is within me. Bless his holy name.*

Psalms 103:2, *Bless the Lord, O my soul, and forget not all his benefits.*

Psalms 103:22, *Bless the Lord, all his works in all places of his dominion: bless the Lord, O my soul.*

Psalms 104:1, *Bless the Lord, O my soul, O Lord my God, thou art very great; thou art clothed with honor and majesty.*

Psalms 134:2, *Lift up your hands in the sanctuary, and bless the Lord. Bless the Lord thy God for the good land, which he hath given thee. Bless the Lord your God forever and ever: and blessed be thy glorious name, which is exalted above all blessing and praise.*

Revelation 12:11, *And they overcame him by the blood of the Lamb, and by the word of their testimony; and they loved not their lives unto the death.*

Who Is God to You?

Is He your Most High God, All sufficient One, Master, Lord of Peace, the Lord Who Will Provide? Is He your Father? We must be careful not to make God into an "it" or a "thing" to which we pray. He is our Jehovah Raah, the Lord our Shepherd. God knows us by our name. Shouldn't we know Him by His?

Hallowed Be Your Name

To hallow a thing is to make it holy or to set it apart to be exalted as being worthy of absolute devotion. To hallow the name of God is to regard Him with complete devotion and loving admiration. God's name is of the utmost importance. Therefore we ought to reserve Him a position of grave significance in our minds and hearts. We should never take His name lightly but always rejoice in it and think deeply upon its true meaning.

We Hallow God's Name:

- With our lips when all our conversation is holy and we speak of those things which are meant to minister grace to the hearers.

- In our thoughts when we suppress every rising evil emotion and have our tempers regulated by His grace and Spirit.

- In our lives when we begin, continue and end our works to His glory. If we have an eye to God in all we perform then every act of our common employment will be an act of religious worship.

- In our families when we endeavor to bring up our children in the discipline and admonition of the Lord; instructing also our servants in the way of righteousness.

- In a particular calling or business when we separate the falsity, deception and lying, commonly practiced, from it; buying and selling as in the sight of the holy and just God.[1]

Decree His Name

As you decree these hallowed holy names of God, think about what each name is and the power that is in that name. So when you say, "I worship You" you are worshipping that attribute of what that name represents and not just speaking it. In each name is a part of His character and nature. So worship Him with every part of your being as you speak these awesome Holy and powerful names of God. As you speak His nature and character it will come alive in you in a deep and profound way.

Let us speak His holy name into the atmosphere and swallow up all the ungodly words that will be spoken about our God!

You Are:

Elohim, the Creator of all, and I worship You.

El-Shaddai, the God of almighty blessings, and I worship You.

---

[1] Source: Adam Clarke's Commentary on the Bible

Adonai, You are my Lord and my master, the complete and self-existent one and I worship You.

Jehova-Jireh, You are my provider and I worship You.

Jehova-Raph, You are my healer and I worship You.

Jehova-M'kaddesh, You are my sanctification and I worship You.

Jehova-Nissi, You are my banner, my victory, my vindication and I worship You.

Jehova-Shalom, You are my peace and I worship You.

Jehova-Tsidkenu, You are my righteousness and I worship You.

Jehova-Rohi, You are my shepherd and I worship You.

Jehova-Shamma, You are the God who is always there and I worship You.

Jehova-El-Elyon, You are the highest God who is the first cause of everything and I worship You.

Jehovah-God, I exalt Your name above all other names. There is no other name like You, Jesus! I worship You.

The Names of Jesus in the Book of Revelation

You are the First-born from the dead and I worship You.
(Revelation 1:5)

You are the highest of earthly kings and I worship You.
(Revelation 1:5)

You are the Alpha and Omega and I worship You.
(Revelation 1:8)

You are the Lord God and I worship You. (Revelation 1:8)

You are the Almighty and I worship You. (Revelation 1:8)

You are the Son of Man and I worship You. (Revelation 1:13)

You are the First and the Last and I worship You.
(Revelation 1:7, 1:11,21:6, 22:130

You are the Living One and I worship You. (Revelation 1:18)

You are the Son of God and I worship You. (Revelation 2:18)

You are the Witness, the Faithful Witness, and I worship You.
(Revelation 3:14)

You are the Creator and I worship You. (Revelation 4:11)

You are the Lion of the Tribe of Judah and I worship You.
(Revelation 5:5)

You are the Root of David and I worship You.
(Revelation 5:5)

You are the Lamb and I worship You. (Revelation 5:6)

You are the Shepherd and I worship You. (Revelation 7:17)

You are the Christ the Anointed One and I worship You.
(Revelation 12:10)

You are Faithful and True and I worship You. (Revelation 19:11)

You are the Word of God and I worship You.
(Revelation 19:13)

You are the King of Kings and I worship You.
(Revelation 19:16)

You are the Lord of Lords and I worship You.
(Revelation 19:16)

Whatever word you use when you call upon the name of God, always remember to call in reverence and in love for the word that expresses the essence of God in His most intimate relationship with you is LOVE-for God is love (1 John 4:16c).

We are waiting for Yahweh; He is our help and our shield, For in Him our heart rejoices, In His holy name we trust. Yahweh, let your faithful love rest on us. As our hope has rested in you.

Psalm 30:22

Chapter 23
DECREEING THE ONE
ANOTHER SCRIPTURES

*Leviticus 19:11, "'Do not steal. "'Do not lie. "' Do not deceive one
another.*

*Zechariah 7:9, This is what the Lord Almighty says: "Administer
true justice; show mercy and compassion to one another."*

*John 13:14, Now that I, your Lord and Teacher, have washed your
feet, you also should wash one another's feet.*

*John 13:34, A new command I give you: Love one another. As I
have loved you, so you must love one another.*

*John 13:35, By this all men will know that you are my disciples, if
you love one another."*

*Romans 12:10, Be devoted to one another in brotherly love. Honor
one another above yourselves.*

Note: All Scriptures in this chapter are taken from the New International
Version Bible (NIV) unless otherwise noted.

Romans 12:16, Live in harmony with one another. Do not be proud, but be willing to associate with people of low position. Do not be conceited.

Romans 13:8, Let no debt remain outstanding, except the continuing debt to love one another, for he who loves his fellowman has fulfilled the law.

Romans 14:13, Therefore let us stop passing judgment on one another. Instead, make up your mind not to put any stumbling block or obstacle in your brother's way.

Romans 15:7, Accept one another, then, just as Christ accepted you, in order to bring praise to God.

Romans 16:16, Greet one another with a holy kiss. All the churches of Christ send greetings.

1 Corinthians 1:10, I appeal to you, brothers, in the name of our Lord Jesus Christ, that all of you agree with one another so that there may be no divisions among you and that you may be perfectly united in mind and thought.

1 Corinthians 16:20, All the brothers here send you greetings. Greet one another with a holy kiss.

2 Corinthians 13:12, Greet one another with a holy kiss.

Galatians 5:13, You, my brothers, were called to be free. But do not use your freedom to indulge the sinful nature; rather, serve one another in love.

Ephesians 4:2, Be completely humble and gentle; be patient, bearing with one another in love.

Ephesians 4:32, Be kind and compassionate to one another, forgiving each other, just as in Christ God forgave you.

Ephesians 5:19, Speak to one another with psalms, hymns and spiritual songs. Sing and make music in your heart to the Lord.

Ephesians 5:21, Submit to one another out of reverence for Christ.

Colossians 3:13, Bear with each other and forgive whatever grievances you may have against one another. Forgive as the Lord forgave you.

Colossians 3:16, Let the word of Christ dwell in you richly as you teach and admonish one another with all wisdom, and as you sing psalms, hymns and spiritual songs with gratitude in your hearts to God.

1 Thessalonians 5:11, Therefore encourage one another and build each other up, just as in fact you are doing.

Hebrews 3:13, But encourage one another daily, as long as it is called Today, so that none of you may be hardened by sin's deceitfulness (NIV)

Hebrews 10:24, And let us consider how we may spur one another on toward love and good deeds.

Hebrews 10:25, [Let us not give] up meeting together, as some are in the habit of doing, but let us encourage one another – and all the more as you see the Day approaching.

James 4:11, Brothers, do not slander one another. Anyone who speaks against his brother or judges him speaks against the law and judges it. When you judge the law, you are not keeping it, but sitting in judgment on it.

1 Peter 1:22, Now that you have purified yourselves by obeying the truth so that you have sincere love for your brothers, love one another deeply, from the heart.

1 Peter 3:8 (ISV), Finally, all of you, live in harmony with one another; be sympathetic, love as brothers, be compassionate and humble.

1 Peter 4:9, Offer hospitality to one another without grumbling.

1 Peter 5:5, Young men, in the same way be submissive to those who are older. All of you, clothe yourselves with humility toward one another, because, "God opposes the proud but gives grace to the humble."

1 Peter 5:14, Greet one another with a kiss of love. Peace to all of you who are in Christ.

1 John 1:7, But if we walk in the light, as he is in the light, we have fellowship with one another, and the blood of Jesus, his Son, purifies us from all sin.

1 John 3:11, This is the message you heard from the beginning: We should love one another.

1 John 3:23, And this is his command: to believe in the name of his Son, Jesus Christ, and to love one another as he commanded us.

1 John 4:7, Dear friends, let us love one another, for love comes from God. Everyone who loves has been born of God and knows God.

1 John 4:11, Dear friends, since God so loved us, we also ought to love one another.

1 John 4:12, No one has ever seen God; but if we love one another, God lives in us and his love is made complete in us.

2 John 1:5, And now, dear lady, I am not writing you a new command but one we have had from the beginning. I ask that we love one another.

Chapter 24
I AM & I HAVE DECREES

I am complete in Him Who is the Head of all principality and power. (Colossians 2:10)

I am alive with Christ. (Ephesians 2:5)

I am free from the law of sin and death. (Romans 8:2)

I am far from oppression and fear does not come near me. (Isaiah 54:14)

I am born of God, and the evil one does not touch me. (1 John 5:18)

I am holy and without blame before Him in love. (Ephesians 1:4; 1 Peter 1:16)

I have the mind of Christ. (1 Corinthians 2:16; Philippians 2:5)

I have the peace of God that passes all understanding.
(Philippians 4:7)

I have the Greater One living in me; greater is He Who is in me
than he who is in the world. (1 John 4:4)

I have received the gift of righteousness and reign as a king in life
by Jesus Christ. (Romans 5:17)

I have received the spirit of wisdom and revelation in the
knowledge of Jesus; the eyes of my understanding being
enlightened. (Ephesians 1:17-18)

I have received the power of the Holy Spirit to lay hands on the
sick and see them recover, to cast out demons, to speak with
new tongues. I have power over all the power of the enemy, and
nothing shall by any means harm me. (Mark 16:17-18; Luke
10:17-19)

I have put off the old man and have put on the new man, which
is renewed in the knowledge after the image of Him Who created
me. (Colossians 3:9-10)

I have given, and it is given to me; good measure, pressed down,
shaken together, and running over, men give into my bosom.
(Luke 6:38)

I have no lack for my God supplies all of my need according to His riches in glory by Christ Jesus. (Philippians 4:19)

I can quench all the fiery darts of the wicked one with my shield of faith. (Ephesians 6:16)

I can do all things through Christ Jesus. (Philippians 4:13)

I show forth the praises of God Who has called me out of darkness into His marvelous light. (1 Peter 2:9)

I am God's child for I am born again of the incorruptible seed of the Word of God, which lives and abides forever. (1 Peter 1:23)

I am God's workmanship, created in Christ unto good works (Ephesians 2:10).

I am a new creature in Christ. (2 Corinthians 5:17)

I am a spirit being alive to God.
(Romans 6:11;1 Thessalonians 5:23)

I am a believer and the light of the Gospel shines in my mind.
(2 Corinthians 4:4)

I am a doer of the Word and blessed in my actions.
(James 1:22,25)

I am a joint-heir with Christ. (Romans 8:17)

I am more than a conqueror through Him Who loves me.
(Romans 8:37)

I am an overcomer by the Blood of the Lamb and the word of my
testimony. (Revelation 12:11)

I am firmly rooted, built up, established in my faith and
overflowing with gratitude. (Colossians 2:7)

I am an ambassador for Christ. (2 Corinthians 5:20)

I am part of a chosen generation, a royal priesthood, a holy
nation and a purchased people. (1 Peter 2:9)

I am the righteousness of God in Jesus Christ.
(2 Corinthians 5:21)

I am the temple of the Holy Spirit; I am not my own. (1
Corinthians 6:19)

I am a partaker of His divine nature (2 Peter 1:3-4).

I am the head and not the tail; I am above only and not beneath. (Deuteronomy 28:13)

I am the light of the world. (Matthew 5:14).

I am His elect, full of mercy, kindness, and humility and longsuffering. (Romans 8:33; Colossians 3:12)

I am forgiven of all my sins and washed in the Blood. (Ephesians 1:7)

I am delivered from the power of darkness and translated into God's Kingdom. (Colossians 1:13)

I am redeemed from the curse of sin, sickness, and poverty. (Deuteronomy 28:15-68; Galatians 3:13)

I am called of God to be the voice of His praise. (Psalm 66:8; 2 Timothy 1:9)

I am healed by the stripes of Jesus. (Isaiah 53:5; 1 Peter 2:24)

I am raised up with Christ and seated in heavenly places. (Ephesians 2:6; Colossians 2:12)

I am greatly loved by God. (Romans 1:7; Ephesians 2:4; Colossians 3:12; 1 Thessalonians 1:4)

I am strengthened with all might according to His glorious power. (Colossians 1:11)

I am submitted to God, and the devil flees from me because I resist him in the Name of Jesus. (James 4:7)

I press on toward the goal to win the prize to which God in Christ Jesus is calling us upward. (Philippians 3:14)

For God has not given us a spirit of fear; but of power, love, and a sound mind. (2 Timothy 1:7)

It is not I who live, but Christ lives in me. (Galatians 2:20)

I am!

Chapter 25
DECREES FOR FAVOR

Favor Declarations

I am blessed and highly favored with God and man because I am truthful, loyal and kind, and I hide the Word of God in my heart; I wear it like a necklace around my neck. I know Favor is not fair - but I am favored of the Lord and I walk in Favor!

The Favor of God is operating and functioning in my life. It surrounds my life like a shield. His Favor goes before me and prepares my way. Favor opens doors for me that no man can open and blessings and opportunity are flooding my life, business and ministry.

I have Favor with my family, friends, on my job, in my business, in my ministry, and in all my relationships, with everyone I come in contact with whether in person or on the phone. All my endeavors are blessed of the Lord and favored. God's blessings and Favor come to me each and every day.

Whatever I set my hand to touch prospers and succeeds because of His Favor on my life. God's favor brings promotion and increase to my life and everything the devil has stolen from me he has to return seven times because I am favored and I am a child of the Most High God.

God's Favor fills my life with overflowing blessing, peace, joy, fulfillment and abundance. God's Favor takes me where my own ability and wisdom cannot.

Wonderful things are always happening to me, so it's a sure thing that something good is going to happen to me today!

Never let loyalty and kindness leave you! Tie them around your neck as a reminder. Write them deep within your heart. Then you will find favor with both God and people, and you will earn a good reputation. (Proverbs 3:3-4 NLT)

A good man obtains favor of the Lord; but a man of wicked devises will he condemn. (Proverbs 12:2 KJV)

When a man's ways please the Lord, he makes even his enemies to be at peace with him. (Proverbs 16:7 KJV)

For thou, Lord, will bless the righteous; with favor with you compass him as a shield. (Psalm 5:12 KJV)

I know thy works: behold, I have set before you an open door, and no man can shut it. (Revelation 3:8 KJV)

I declare I am God's favorite

Favor Goes Before Me

I declare the Favor of God goes before me today; it is in my past; it is in my present; it is in my future. I declare Jesus Christ, the same yesterday, today and forever, is perfect and unchangeable. He always has been; He always will be. He is my Savior. I declare Holy Spirit guides me into favorable pathways.

I declare the Favor of God – the goodness and mercy twins – follows after me even through the valley of the shadow of death. I declare the Favor of God is preservation to my right and on my left for the destroyer falling a thousand at my side and ten thousand at my right hand will not come near me. I declare the Favor of God is below my feet as a sure, well-lit pathway of firm stepping-stones. I declare the Favor of God is above my head as a cloud of protection by day and a glory flame of fire by night.

I declare the Favor of God saturates me, for Christ goes before me and after me; in me and on me; below me, above me and through me.

Imagination and Extravagance

I declare my imagination is under the authority of the Word of God. My thoughts favor others and myself for Christ is in my thoughts. I take captive every imagination to the obedience of Christ. I recognize the power within me, believing I can have whatsoever I can think on or ask for.

I choose to think on things that edify and encourage. I choose to think on things that are exceeding abundantly beyond my natural expectation or capability of achieving. If I can imagine it, God is way beyond it. I stretch my imagination to think big, bold thoughts that make me tremble for if I do not tremble at the extravagant heart of my Father, I do diminish Him.

I choose to believe in an exponentially magnificent Father who loves me extravagantly, has every resource at his disposal for Kingdom expansion through me, and whose generosity toward me knows no limitation. The Word of God renews my mind for I have the mind of Christ.

Emotions and Renewing the Mind

I declare my emotions bring Favor to myself and to others for I yield my emotions to Christ. I flow with emotions that favor righteousness, joy and peace in the Holy Spirit. I take authority over my emotions bringing them into submission to the eternal will of the Father.

I choose to command my emotions rather than have my emotions command me.

I bind emotions that would strike out to kill, steal, and destroy. I loose emotions so Christ's abundant life flows through all that I think and feel, say and do.

I declare my words are Holy Spirit anointed words favoring myself and others for Christ is in my words; I speak only what I hear the Father say setting a watch before my lips that I might not speak against the heart of God.

I Choose Godly Actions, Favor and Grace

I declare my actions are aligned with the Will of God bringing favor on all whom I touch today. My actions display the Favor of God; my actions are aligned with Christ who is aligned with the Father who is full of faithfulness and mercy and compassion.

I choose to walk in mercy for mercy triumphs over judgment. I am called to have dominion over natural elements and generosity towards people. Today, I choose to excel in the grace of giving. I choose to see the best in those with whom I mix and mingle. I choose to speak the best about those with whom I have relationship. I choose to loose the best for those in authority over me both politically and spiritually. I choose actions that will bring Favor on those who trespass against me. I choose actions that release the flow of God's Favor in the world through me.

I choose the Favor of God today. I choose to receive God's Favor. I choose to flow with God's Favor. I choose to believe that God is a good God and that Our Heavenly Father has immeasurable Favor stored up for the righteous. I tap into Favor that lies dormant in my family line. I draw from Heaven's storehouse the Favor that is laid up for previous generations of my family not yet withdrawn. I respond to the open door and the heartfelt invitation to "come up here." By faith, I reach into the heavenlies catching God's view of His extravagant love for the family of man. I draw on my heavenly account believing that my God-given dreams have magnificent resources in Heaven to bank roll manifestation in the earth. I declare as in Heaven so on earth.

I choose to be a conduit of Favor for future generations. I look hundreds of years into the future, should Jesus tarry, believing that Favor will flow to and through my family so mankind is blessed in each generation. I believe my family line has Favor with the Father. I believe my family line will bless and not curse. I believe my family line will be the head and not the tail. I believe God has a destiny for each member of my family to a thousand generations of those that love Him.

Today I choose the Favor of God. I choose to think on it. I choose emotions that support it.

I choose to speak of it. I choose to act on it.

I choose the Favor of God in every circumstance, realizing Favor sometimes appears as momentary disfavor only to be proven later as providential Favor sparing me from deep disappointment and long-lasting disfavor.

Today, I choose God's Favor declaring, it will have first place in my mind, my heart, my soul and my strength. I choose God's Favor for my neighbor as I choose it for myself.

I choose Favor because I choose the Father, the Son, and the Holy Spirit as my One-True God to whom I pledge my absolute fidelity. I declare I am God's favorite!

Proclamation of Favor

In the Name of Jesus, I am the righteousness of God; Therefore, I am entitled to covenant kindness and Favor. The Favor of

God is among the righteous. His Favor surrounds the righteous; therefore it surrounds me everywhere I go, everything I do,

I expect the Favor of God to be in manifestation and never again will I be without the Favor of God.

Satan, my days in Lodebar, a place of barrenness, cease today. I am leaving that place of lack and want. I am going from the pit to the palace because the Favor of God is on me.

It rests richly on me. It profusely abounds in me, and I am part of the generation that will experience the Favor of God, immeasurable, limitless, and surpassing.

Therefore, God's Favor produces in my life supernatural increase, promotion, prominence, preferential treatment, restoration, honor, increased assets, great victories, recognition, petitions granted, policies and rules changed on my behalf, and battles won that I don't have to fight.

The favor of God is upon me, and it goes before me; my life will never be the same. In Jesus' name, Amen

Chapter 26
EVERYDAY DECREES & DECLARATIONS

Declarations: 1

(Romans 4:17, Romans 10:9-10)

These ten basic declarations are foundational to the building of your faith. They will increase expectancy of God's goodness; and, thus, will increase the manifestation of that goodness in your life. Jesus said. *"According to your faith, so be it"* (Matthew 8:13). Say these (and the other declarations lists) every day for a month and see what happens to your life.

1. My prayers are powerful and effective.
(2 Corinthians 5:21, James 5:16b)

2. God richly supplies all my financial needs. (Philippians 4:19)

3. I am dead to sin and alive to obeying God. (Romans 6:11)

4. I walk in ever-increasing health. (Isaiah 53:3-5,
Psalm 103:1-3)

5. I live under a supernatural protection. (Psalm 91)

6. I prosper in all my relationships. (Luke 2:52)

7. I consistently bring God encounters to other people. (Mark 16:17,180

8. Through Jesus I am 100% loved and worthy to receive all of God's blessings. (Galatians 3:1-5)

9. Each of my family members is wonderfully blessed and radically loves Jesus. (Acts 16:30,31)

10. I laugh uproariously when I hear a lie from the devil. (Psalm 2:2-4)

Declarations: 2

Remember this: faith is the evidence of things not seen (Hebrews 11:1). Our 'evidence' for things being true is not our circumstances, but God's promises. We don't deny negative facts in our lives, but we choose to focus on a higher reality: God's truth. Faith indeed comes by hearing (Romans 10:17); therefore, we choose to speak these powerful truths to build our own faith.

1. I set the course of my life with my declarations (James 3:2-5)

2. God is on my side; therefore I declare that I cannot be defeated, discouraged, depressed or disappointed. (Romans 8:37, Psalms 91, Philippians 4:13)

3. I am the head and not the tail. I have insight and I have wisdom. I have ideas and divine strategies. I have authority. (Deuteronomy 28:13, Deuteronomy 8:18, James 1:5-8, Luke 10:19)

4. As I speak God's promises, they come to pass. They stop all attacks, assaults, oppression, and fear from my life. (2 Peter 1:2-4, Mark 11:23-24)

5. I have the wisdom of God today. I will think the right thoughts, say the right words, and make the right decisions in every situation I face. (James 1:5,1 Corinthians 2:16)

6. I expect to have powerful divine appointments today to heal the sick, to raise the dead, to prophesy life, to lead people to Christ, to bring deliverance, to release signs and wonders and to bless every place I go. (the book of Acts)

7. I expect the best day of my life spiritually, emotionally, relationally, and financially in Jesus' Name. (Romans 15:13)

Declarations: 3

One of the main 'methods' Jesus and the apostles used (in the gospels and Acts) was to SPEAK TO things, You will notice that they did not ask God to heal people, to cast out demons, or to raise the dead; but they spoke to bodies, to demons, to the wind, etc. Jesus encouraged us to speak to mountains in Mark 11:23. This set of declarations focuses much on our speaking to the various aspects in our lives.

1. I have a covenant with God, and by the Blood of Jesus I release my divine protection and divine provision. (Hebrews 8:6)

2. My angels are carrying out the Word of God on my behalf. (Psalm 103:20)

3. Any adversity, attack, accidents and tragedies that were headed my way are diverted right now in Jesus' Name. (Psalm 91)

4. I speak to the raging waters in my life; peace, be still. I say to my mind; peace, be still. I say to my emotions; peace, be still. I say to my body; peace, be still. I say to my home; peace, be still. I say to my family; peace, be still. (Mark 4:39)

5. Now I speak to every mountain of fear, every mountain of discouragement, every mountain of stress, every mountain of depression, every mountain of lack and insufficiency; and I say, "Be removed and cast into the sea in Jesus' Name!" (Mark 11:22-24)

6. And I speak to this day and I call You blessed. And I declare that I serve a mighty God who today will do exceedingly and abundantly beyond all that I can ask or think (Ephesians 3:20). I say You are a good God and I eagerly anticipate Your goodness today. And finally, I declare that I don't have to be able to understand it or work it all out for God to be able to do it! In Jesus' Name.

Declarations: 4

1. I live a victorious life and I am part of a victorious church.

2. God's Promises are true for me and for everything I do.

3. God will abundantly supply all my needs in every way this year.

4. God is good all the time.

5. The wrath and judgments of God were poured out on Jesus so that His goodness could be poured out on me, and God's kindness leads to repentance.

Chapter 27

DECREE & TEAR DOWN STRONGHOLDS

I decree & declare that we are all sufficient in Jesus Christ's sufficiency.

I decree & declare that we have put on the whole Armor of God.

I decree and declare that we are well able to stand against the wiles and trickeries of the devil.

I decree and declare that we have dominion over principalities, powers, rulers of darkness of this age, and over spiritual hosts of wickedness in the heavenly places.

I decree and declare that the Greater One lives in me.

I decree and declare that I am the temple of God.

I decree and declare that my mouth is a weapon that speaks the uncompromising, unstoppable word of the Living God.

I decree and declare that what I say comes to pass and never returns void.

I decree and declare that every spirit and stronghold of satan assigned to me, my family and my church must come down now, in the Name of Jesus.

I decree and declare that the curse of the Law is broken over me and my family and my church.

I decree and declare that every hidden stronghold and evil spirit is revealed and loosed from my family, my church and me.

I decree and declare that I am submitted to God and put Him first, and therefore Satan must flee from me.

I decree and declare that I have closed every door and satan has no entrance into me, my family, my business or my ministry

I decree and declare that the Name of Jesus, Jesus, Jesus, Jesus is lifted high by my life of prayer, praise and righteousness.

I decree and declare that I am a winner and everything that I pray for in line with the will of God is mine now, in Jesus' name.

Chapter 28
DECREE AS A CHILD OF GOD

I decree and declare, God, You granted me/us supernatural strength and ability to fight the good fight of faith.

I decree and declare I am qualified to share in Jesus' inheritance.

I decree and declare I am a representative of God.

I decree and declare I am firmly rooted, built up and established in the faith.

I decree and declare I am a steward of great wealth.

I decree and declare I am a follower of Christ, the Light of the world.

I decree and declare healing power flows in me to lay hands on the sick and they shall recover.

I decree and declare that I am anointed by God.

I decree and declare there is a hedge of protection around me.

I decree and declare that I will never be broke another day in my life.

I decree and declare God has provided for me wisdom, knowledge and understanding.

I decree and declare that God will bless me with multiple streams of income.

I decree and declare God will bless me with multiple multi-million dollar ideas, inventions and strategies.

I decree and declare I am God's representative in the earth realm.

I decree and declare God gives me authority and power to expose Satan's tactics and overcome his attacks.

I decree and declare no weapon formed against me shall prosper.

I decree and declare that I am healed by the stripes of Jesus Christ from the crown on my head to the soles of my feet.

I announce that it is You, God, that has blessed me. It is You, God, that has the power over me.

It's not by our might nor by our power but by the Spirit of the Lord.

When the enemy comes in, like a flood You lift up a standard against them.

This is the Word of the Lord, In Jesus' name. Amen.

DECREE YOUR TODAY!

DECREE YOUR TODAY!

192

Chapter 29

DECREES OF HIS WORD & GOODNESS

I declare today that God is good, that the Word of God stands forever.

I choose today to stay with Jesus and His Word, and to see Him perform His Word on my behalf.

He has exalted His Name and His Word and He has magnified His Word even above His great Name, therefore I choose and declare today that I stand in 100% agreement with Your Words.

I choose to give Your Word the same degree of importance in my life that You do.

You gave me Your Words and I receive them.

Your Word is a lamp to my feet and a light to my path.

Your Word is a fire shut up in my bones so I release the fire of Your Word by decree and declaration.

Your Word is LIFE to those who find them and healing to all their flesh.

Your Word is a sword which cuts through my joints and heals them.

Your Word sorts out the thoughts, attitudes and intentions of my heart.

Your Word cleans up the very blood marrow inside my bones and gives me wellbeing through new stem cells.

Your Word heals and delivers from destruction.

Your Word saves to the uttermost.

Your Word is near me; it is in my mouth.

Your Word prospers in all the places it is declared and absolutely does not return to You empty, but fulfills its purpose.

All of Your promises are Yes and Amen in Christ Jesus the Anointed One

Your promises – Your Word – teaches me to be diligent.

Your Word contains everything I need to live a life of Godliness, which brings glory to God.

Your Word gives me the knowledge to be morally excellent, develop Christian energy, develop intelligence, develop self-control, and develop steadfastness and patience.

Your Word works in me, exercising me to brotherly love and affection.

I declare that I absolutely love Your Word, because it came from Your Father to me.

I decree this day that God is a Good God and is the God of all Goodness.

Father, Son and Holy Spirit created me in their likeness and image and called me Good.

I was wonderfully fashioned together in my Mother's womb by the design of God- He called me Good.

By the power if the Holy Spirit I have been made into a new creation on the inside.

I am living proof of the Goodness of God.

He planned all the days of my life before ever one of them came into being and His plans for me are Good.

He plans to continually prosper me and my future is full of hope and Goodness.

Every circumstance that appears to be against me – You, God, cause to turn for my Good – You always bring an outcome of Goodness.

How great is Your Goodness, which You have laid up for those who reverence You with awe and wonder and who worship You. This goodness is Yours, which You have formed and worked into the life and heart of those who trust and take refuge in You.

I am satisfied with Your Goodness in my life which is Your temple.

I will declare Your greatness and my mouth will pour forth like a fountain the fame of Your Goodness and sing aloud of Your rightness and justice.

How great is Your Goodness and how great is Your beauty and how great You will make my Goodness and my beauty.

I am becoming more and more a reflection of His Goodness.

Your Goodness leads me to change my mind and my ways and causes me to come into agreement with Your Good will and purpose for my life.

The Goodness of God influences me to be a great giver to the poor, to do deeds of kindness and justice and goodness – these things will endure and go on forever and ever.

The effect of Your Goodness produces in my life an upright heart and trueness of life.

I am rich in Your Goodness and amply filled with spiritual knowledge; therefore I can continually and purposefully declare the Goodness of God in the land of the Living-

Surely Goodness and Mercy shall follow me all the days of my life and I shall dwell in Your Presence forever.

Chapter 30

DECREES OF PROSPERITY & PROVISION

I seek first the Kingdom of God and His righteousness, and all the things I need are added unto me.

I do not fear because it is my Father's good pleasure to give me the Kingdom.

I acknowledge that Christ Jesus meets all my needs according to God's riches in glory. Grace and Peace are multiplied unto me through the knowledge of God and of Jesus my Lord.

His divine power has given me all things that pertain to life and godliness, through the knowledge of Him that has called me to glory and virtue.

Blessed be the God and Father of my Lord Jesus Christ, who has blessed me with every spiritual blessing in the heavenly places in Christ.

The Lord is Sun and a Shield to me and will give me grace and glory.

No good thing will He withhold from me as I walk uprightly.

By the power of the Blood of Jesus, I claim and declare complete health and a prosperous path in all things even as my soul prospers.

All my paths drip with His anointing and my year is crowned with His bounty.

Shout for joy at His righteous cause, be glad and continually decree.

Let the Lord be magnified who has pleasure in the prosperity of His servant.

Through Christ Jesus the blessing promised to Abraham is mine, and through the powerful working of the Holy Spirit the blessings become reality.

I give to the Lord, to His people and to the needy as I purpose in my heart to give.

I choose to sow bountifully; therefore I will reap bountifully.

I do not give grudgingly or out of compulsion, for my God loves a cheerful giver.

God makes all grace abound towards me.

I always have enough for all things, so that I may abound to every good work.

The Lord supplies seed for me to sow and bread for my food.

He multiplies my seed for sowing and increases the fruit of my righteousness.

I am enriched in everything unto great abundance, which brings much thanksgiving to God.

I bring all my tithes into the Lord's storehouse, so that there is meat in His house. As a result He opens the windows of Heaven and pours out a blessing for me so that there is not room to contain it.

I remember the Lord my God, for it is He who gives me the power to make wealth that He may confirm His covenant.

Because Jesus Christ my Savior diligently listened to the voice of God and obeyed all the commandments, the Lord will set me high above all the nations of the earth and all the blessings in the Kingdom shall come upon me and overtake me.

Christ became poor so that through His poverty I might become rich.

Jesus came so that I would have life in its abundance;

I am very blessed and favored of God and have been called to be blessing to others.

Chapter 31
DECREES AS
AN OVERCOMER

I decree and declare to enter into Your holy throne by the Blood
of Jesus that He has consecrated for me.

I decree with a true heart and full assurance of faith to draw near
to God and hunger for His heart of Love.

I decree The Kingdom of God is actively responding to my
desires as Christ gives me the desires of my heart.

I decree with the authority of both King and Priest according to
Your Word!

I decree that my words are empowered and emanate the Holy
Spirit and will never return to me void.

I decree that I am covered by the Blood of Jesus.
I make this decree that
I AM AN OVERCOMER!!

I decree that I have overcome all fear, doubt, unbelief, demonic influences, word curses, unfruitful relationships, poverty, sickness, failures, past events, and worthless thinking by the Blood of the lamb and the words of my testimony.

I decree that I have the mind of Christ and the helmet of salvation covers my mind.

I decree that I triumph in Christ. For Christ has provided a way of escape from all temptation and I joyfully walk through the door.

I decree My loving father will not allow me to be tempted beyond my abilities. God goes with me, fighting for me against my enemies, causing them to fail. Man can do nothing to me because I trust wholeheartedly in Christ.

I decree that I am neither afraid nor discouraged because God has given me the spirit of a warrior and I always succeed.

I decree I overcome all powers of darkness. Nothing is able to harm me. No weapon designed to attack me or discourage me will prosper.

I decree that every plan and word released against me will fail.

I decree I am engulfed in the unfailing love of God my Father. The Spirit of God raises a standard against the negatives that try to flood my life. Goodness and mercy forever follow me.

I decree that when then enemy comes in, like a flood the Lord will rise up in me and make me a standard that will demonstrate the power and authority of God for Kingdom advancement.

I decree that I am created like God in holiness and righteousness.

I decree that the spirit of my mind is new. I am divinely and clothed and covered in my new self.

I decree the old negative image of myself is dead, buried and gone.

I decree I am fearfully and wonderfully made in the image of God.

I decree to let go of any limited thoughts of the presence of God within me and release the hands of God to work in my life.

I decree that the presence of God in me is greater than the presence of the enemy in the world.

I decree I have overcome the systems of the world, the world's mentality, and the world's ethics because the greater presence of God is in me.

I decree to boldly resist Satan and surrender and submit to God's Kingdom system.

I decree NOW that the Kingdom of God is activated in me NOW! The Kingdom of Heaven is activated in me NOW! The Kingdom of Righteousness peace and joy is activated in me NOW! The heart of the King is activated in me NOW! The Kingdom of God is activated in me NOW!

I decree my inner man is established on the words of Christ, and the gates of hell will not prevail against it.

I decree my thought life has overcome because my mind is cleansed from an evil conscience.

I decree I have overcome all guilt and shame of my past. I decree shame off me, it has no place in my life!

I decree that I possess a fearless heart because divine intelligence provides every solution.

I decree like Caleb I am well able to overcome my giants. I decree like David I shout my decrees back at the giants of life.

I am an overcomer and the plan and purpose of God is rising up with in me like fire shut up in my bones. I overcome by the Blood of the Lamb and the word of these decrees.

I am an OVERCOMER!

Chapter 32
DECREES OF LIFE

I decree I am the Body of Christ. My body is the house of God. God lives in me and I belong to Him. I've been bought with the price of the Blood of Jesus, so I glorify God in my body and in my spirit.

I decree Satan has no power over me. I have been delivered from the power of darkness and translated into the Kingdom of God's dear Son.

Therefore sin has no power over me.

I separate myself from every unclean thing.

I submit myself to God. I resist the devil and he flees from me.

I decree that I will go into all the world, I will preach the gospel to every creature, I will make disciples, I will cast out devils, I will lay hands on the sick and they do recover, I will speak with new tongue, and if I drink any deadly thing it does not hurt me, because greater is He that is in me than he that is in the world.

I decree that I have the heart of the Father and
I will manifest it to the world.

I decree I give no place or no opportunity to the devil.

I choose the fear of the Lord, which is to hate evil, pride,
arrogance, evil way, and the disobedient mouth.

I consider Jesus and His presence in me.

I decree I love God more than anything this world has to offer.

I present my body as a living sacrifice to God - holy, set apart,
devoted and consecrated to please Him, which is a part of my
spiritual worship to Him.

I am not conformed to this world's way of thinking, but I am
continually being transformed by the renewing of my mind to
His Word so that I can prove what is the good, the acceptable
and the perfect will of God in my life

I decree I have the mind of Christ.

Jesus said, "The enemy of the world comes, but he has nothing in
Me." Just like Jesus, I decree that Satan has nothing in me.

I cast down imaginations and every thought that tries to exalt itself against the knowledge of God. I bring my thoughts into captivity to the obedience of Christ and His Word - having a ready mind to revenge all disobedience.

I decree I think on things that are true, honest, just, pure, lovely, and of good report. If there be any virtue or praise, I think on these things.

In righteousness I am established. I am far from oppression. I do not fear. I am far from terror. It will not come near me.

Thy Word have I hid in my heart that I might not sin against Thee.

If I sin You said if I confess and repent of my sin, You are faithful and just to forgive me of it and to cleanse me from all unrighteousness.

I decree no weapon formed against me shall prosper and every tongue that rises against me is condemned or shown to be wrong and stopped. This is the heritage God has given me as a servant of the Lord and my righteousness is of Him.

Like Jesus, I love righteousness and I hate iniquity; therefore God anoints me with the oil of gladness.

Lord, You said there is no temptation that has come to me or that can come to me that is not common to man, nothing that is beyond human resistance. You are faithful to Your Word and to Your love for me, and You will not allow me to be tempted beyond my strength to resist, and You will provide a way out or a way of escape so I will be strong against it.

I decree I am of God and I have overcome every anti-Christ spirit because greater is He who is in me than he who is in the world.

This is the victory that causes me to overcome in this world - my faith in Jesus and in His Word.

I decree I live and walk by faith and not by sight or feelings.

I decree I live by every Word that proceeds from the mouth of God.

I decree I let the Word of Christ dwell in me richly in all wisdom.

The spirit of faith is, I believe and therefore I speak.

I decree I overcome the devil by the Blood of the Lamb and by the word of my testimony, not loving my life unto the death.

I decree I shall live and not die and declare the works of the Lord.

All things are working together for good in my life because I love God and I am called according to His purpose.

Thanks be to God who gives me the victory through my Lord Jesus Christ. He always causes me to triumph.

I decree I can do all things through Christ who strengthens me.

Chapter 33

DECREE AND PRAY ISAIAH 61

I decree I am anointed for breakthrough and uncommon victories. Isaiah 61: 1, "The Spirit of the Lord GOD is upon me, because the LORD has anointed me." My natural has put on the SUPERNATURAL.

I decree No obstacle shall be able to stand in my way. Demons and imps that come at me one way shall be scattered seven ways. Because of the BREAKER anointing on me, I am a force to be reckoned with!

Every stronghold is coming down. Every erected altar established against me is coming down! Every wall of offense is coming down! Every camp of war conspiring against me is coming down.

I employ now the BREAKER ANOINTING to break and destroy everything against me, every weapon formed against me now! And it shall be as I have spoken, in the mighty name of Jesus!

I command all gates of witchcraft and all other demonic gates that are designed to prohibit me from receiving and operating in the anointing to be closed NOW that NONE may open, and decree that the Godly gates are now being opened that none may close, in the name of Jesus.

I decree that the anointing within me is now being perpetually unearthed in me and to me, in the name of Jesus.

I decree I tap the anointing within me, step into it, pray it forth, and I decree a mighty stirring of the anointing deep within me now, in the name of Jesus.

I guard, respect and care for my anointing, in the name of Jesus.

I decree my head is anointed with oil, and let my cup run over.

Lord, please anoint, consecrate, and sanctify me as You did Aaron and his sons, that I may minister to You as priest.

Lord, please anoint my eyes with supernatural eye salve that I may see the seen and the unseen.

Lord, release your horn of oil and anoint me for your holy call. Let the Spirit of the Lord come upon me mightily from this day forward.

I decree that I receive the measure of anointing and the fullness of Heaven needed in my life.

I decree that the anointing is now breaking burdens and destroying the yokes of bondage in my life right now, in the name of Jesus.

I decree that the anointing is now placing a perpetual shield around me and is prohibiting any foul thing from penetrating through it, in the name of Jesus.

I decree the Lord is my strength, and He is the saving strength of His anointed.

I decree that God has found me, His servant, and has anointed me with His holy oil, in the name of Jesus.

My horn shall be exalted like the horn of a unicorn: I shall be anointed with fresh oil.

I decree that God has ordained a lamp for me as His anointed, in the name of Jesus.

I decree that He who has established me in Christ and has anointed me is God.

I receive the anointing into my life right now,
in the name of Jesus.

I decree that the anointing that I have received from God abides
in me, and I need not that any man teach me: but the anointing
teaches me all things as I abide in God, and it is truth,
and is no lie.

I decree that I am an anointed vessel of God. The anointing of
God rests upon me, flows into and through me, and into the lives
of others, in the name of Jesus.

Anointing, flow to the very core of my being, in the
name of Jesus.

Anointing, flow mightily through my spirit, in the name of Jesus.

I activate the anointing in my life now, in the name of Jesus.

I decree I am anointed activate things within my spirit, my life,
and in the atmosphere that are lying dormant and need to be
operative right now, in the name of Jesus.

I decree my spirit to come into an ever-increasing knowledge of
the anointing upon my life, in the name of Jesus.

I decree I have Your holy fire; be ignited and burn mightily in my belly right now, in the name of Jesus.

I decree I have anointing fire; rise up and consume me, and flow through the whole of my person, in the name of Jesus.

I decree Your anointing manifest violently, in the name of Jesus.

I decree the anointing bring forth a mighty explosion of power in my life now, in the name of Jesus.

I decree the anointing consume, bombard, and shift the atmosphere around me now, in the name of Jesus.

I decree that the Anointing bombard every yoke in my life and break them now, in the name of Jesus.

I decree my cup is running over NOW with the anointing of God!!! (Praise God here.)

Lord Jesus, please mature me in the anointing.

I decree I am anointed to prosper, excel, and be successful, in the name of Jesus.

I decree that the Spirit of the Lord GOD is upon me, because the LORD has anointed me.

Chapter 34

DECREE YOUR DREAM TODAY

A Dreamer's Prayer of Supplication and Declaration

Father, I adore You and You are worthy to be praised. You are mighty indeed and You alone are glorious. I thank You for giving me dreams birthed from the throne of God into my heart. As I listen to Your heart and hear what the Spirit is saying, I praise You and long for Your will to be done in my life. I will not give up or give in to the tactics of the enemy with reference to Your plans for my life.

I will be of good courage and dream the dreams You have for me. I receive the understanding that I am with You as You are with me to fulfill the visions You place in my heart. I am thankful no one or nothing can stop what You put into motion when it comes to fulfilling my dreams and destiny. I worship You and praise You for the intimacy we have together.

It is in an atmosphere of worshipping You where I receive all the dreams and visions You have for me to receive. I desire only the destiny and purpose You have created me to walk in. Let it unfold and be manifested in my life now and for all eternity.

Lord, what an honor to be Your temple...to be Your plan for spreading the dreams and provisions of Your heart. I will thank You and praise You forever for Your love is indescribable and endures to the very end. I will worship You day and night as I praise You with my whole heart. My greatest dream and desire is for intimate communion and intimacy with You on a continual basis.

Yes, Lord, I am honored to be Your dwelling place...to be a habitation or tent for Your glory. I am one who is filled with Your presence. I am a part of Your plan, as David was, to fulfill Your purpose. Thank You for trusting me with the thoughts and intents of Your heart...for trusting me to be a part of Your dream. I praise You for the reality of participating in the spreading of Your glory on the earth.

You care about all the dreams You have given me. I thank you for making the way for their fulfillment. It is too wonderful to comprehend; yet I will praise You for eternity as I am part of your dream come true. I am a manifest dream of Your heart.

I am in awe that I am a part of Your plan and I praise You for dwelling in me and fulfilling the dreams of my heart. Thank You for the breaker anointing which is making a way right now as I call upon Your name. It is making a way where there is no way, opening doors that cannot be shut, and closing doors that cannot be opened.

Only You can accomplish all things needed to fulfill my dreams Lord. Thank You for being my Way and Way-maker. Today and every day I count on You. You can count on me as I believe big and dream big. You are my all and all. You keep Your Word; therefore, I do trust You with all my heart. I believe You are fulfilling all my dreams. Thank You for giving me the desires of my heart which come from the desires of Your heart.

I bless You Lord, for You are worthy to be praised. I, humbly and with great faith, bless Your Holy name. You are the Potter. I am the clay. As Your vessel, I am ready and willing to be poured out among the people so You may reveal your dreams, visions and passion among men.

As my heart is being cleansed, I praise You, for I am Your workmanship. I am in agreement with You, Lord, and acknowledge I have been made righteous through Your blood to be a vessel of honor.

I long for You to freely express Your heart of dreams through me. Thank You for taking pleasure in me which I will in turn translate by birthing dreams into reality. I declare the work You started in me shall be completed and bring glory to Your name. Truly I will not grow weary in the process. I dare to stretch my tent pegs in order to dream bigger, for I am a co-laborer with You to carry out Your mission on and in the earth.

Lord, I Praise You for truly the dreams and desires of my heart have come from You. I will acknowledge the fact that it is Your promptings in my spirit which move me and motivate me to dream and dream big. I declare that I am obedient to all You desire to do with me and through me. As I acknowledge You in all my ways, You direct my steps to accomplish that which has been planted within the deep recesses of my heart by You.

Thank you for your faithfulness to ignite the passions of my heart to fulfill Your will in the earth. All My dreams originating with You will come to pass as I get into agreement with Your Word to me. Take my dreams to a practical level as I surrender my imagination and reach out to take all You have for me. Help me to make all dreams given by You…inspired by You into a reality. Amen

Chapter 34
MY FINAL THOUGHT

The thoughts contained in this book are the way I will always live my life. Prayerfully some of that fire and zeal in me to decree and declare heavens agenda has jumped on you. I pray that you have been enriched by His word going down deep inside you as you read and declare.

My biggest hope is that as you have read aloud, that you are learning just how vast and deep the heart of God is for you. His very heart and nature and all that He is are captured in these decrees. They are the heart of God, the very nature and existence of who He is. It is how He created the world and how He created you and me. Words! Remember our words have so much power in them that they can either make us or break us, bring life or death. Each time you speak one of these decrees you are bringing Heaven to earth.

I hope that you will use this book each morning to start your day. Remember you decide what your day will be like by the words that you speak – not necessarily the circumstances of the day, rather how you react to them and how God uses you to change them. Today is a good day to decree that "today is a good day."

The Bible says that today is the day of salvation. With your mouth you decree His saving power and with your words you decree His heart to the atmosphere and to the world.

Now you go and make decrees of your love for God! Remember to decree your today, TODAY!

ABOUT THE AUTHOR

"As a prophet of God I have been called to speak, sing, decree, declare, hum and use whatever means possible to decree the heart of God, not just to the world, but also to the atmosphere." ~ Brent Luck

"Expect the unthinkable, believe for the impossible, touch the invisible and see people move out of the natural into the supernatural." This is the heartbeat and passion of Brent's calling – to see God's people move out of limitation and into freedom and embrace the apostolic, prophetic and revolutionary mind-set of the Kingdom. Seeing God's people brought into wholeness to *knowing and demonstrating* their true destiny. Brent declares and sings the transforming power of God. His desire is to see God's people, *"the church"*, move beyond the natural and truly enter into the realm and dimension of the supernatural.

Brent Luck is a powerful preacher, prophet, psalmist, author and recording artist. Previously a professional opera singer, Brent now uses his voice to both sing and proclaim the Glory and Fire of Heaven through decreeing, singing and declaring the Kingdom on earth as it is in Heaven. He ministers in a fiery revival anointing accompanied by revelatory ministry, healing, miracles, signs and wonders. The Lord often uses Brent's accurate prophetic ministry to speak forth individual and corporate vision, to catapult people into their destinies. He and his wife Melissa have a passion to share the love of Christ and to declare "All Things Possible" through the power of prophetically accessing tomorrow, and announcing it today! Brent and Melissa currently serve as itinerant speakers and as part of the leadership team and pastoral staff of XP Shiloh Fellowship. They have three children and live in Maricopa, Arizona.

Contact Information:
Eternal Purpose Ministries
Maricopa, Arizona
www.brentlluck.com
1eternalpurpose.com
brentluck@gmail.com

To order copies of *Decree Your Today* you may connect with the author at www. Brentlluck.com or brentluck@gmail.com

Additional copies of this book and other titles from XP Publishing and XP Ministries are available at the store at Xpministries.com

For wholesale orders for bookstores and ministries please contact:
resourcemanager@xpministries.com

Xpministries.com

Lightning Source UK Ltd.
Milton Keynes UK
UKOW06f1832011015

259696UK00006B/145/P